D1191183

Psychotherapy with Priests, Protestant Clergy, and Catholic Religious
A Practical Guide

Psychotherapy with Priests, Protestant Clergy, and Catholic Religious
A Practical Guide

Joseph W. Ciarrocchi, Ph.D.
Robert J. Wicks, Psy.D.

Loyola College in Maryland

PSYCHOSOCIAL PRESS
MADISON, CONNECTICUT

Copyright © 2000, Psychosocial Press

PSYCHOSOCIAL PRESS® and PSP (& design)® are registered trademarks of International Universities Press, Inc.

All rights reserved. No part of this book may be reproduced by any means, nor translated into a machine language, without the written permission of the publisher.

Library of Congress Cataloging-in-Publication Data

Ciarrocchi, Joseph W.
    Psychotherapy with priests, Protestant clergy, and Catholic religious : a practical guide/
    Joseph W. Ciarrocchi and Robert J. Wicks.
        p. cm.
    Includes bibliographical references.
    ISBN 1-887841-22-9
    1. Clergy—Counseling of. 2. Clergy—Psychology. 3. Christians—Counseling of. 4.
    Pastoral counseling. 5. Psychotherapy. I. Wicks, Robert J. II. Title.

    BV4398.C53 2000
    253.5'2—dc21
                                                                    99-088813

Manufactured in the United States of America

To Anna Marie, with love—JWC

In memory of Reverend Kenneth Wicks.
What he gave to those he served will never be forgotten—RJW

Contents

PART IV: Observing Limits and Handling Change

Introduction

The book's purpose is to enhance the effectiveness of psychotherapy with clergy and Catholic vowed religious. We believe
this requires imparting two interrelated but distinct perspectives. First, we frame counseling with clergy and vowed religious
in a multicultural context. What Allen Bergin (1991) says about
psychotherapy with the religiously committed client, holds doubly true in the treatment of clergy; namely, that a "religiosity
gap" exists between many clinicians and clients.

This gaps exists, as repeated surveys demonstrate, from the
disparity between the personal importance of religion for the
average American, and its lesser importance for mental health
professionals. In concert with Bergin, we conclude that clinical
treatment for intensely religious individuals becomes a multicultural issue, in the same way as therapy with any diverse eth-
nic, racial, or otherwise culturally distinct group.

In order for this book to be helpful from this perspective,
we have framed each relevant psychological issue discussed in
terms of its cultural context for those engaged in professional
ministry. For each issue we will discuss both the social context
that influences the problem, as well as the internal psychological set that either predisposes or complicates the issue. Each
author has had extensive experience in assessment, treatment,
and consultation with these groups, and one of us even trained
and worked within professional ministry.

Second, we approach the assessment, treatment planning, and intervention strategies discussed organically within this multicultural context. We avoid presenting disembodied interventions that pertain to any depressed person, for example. At the same time, therapeutic strategies that have an empirical base shape the interventions we suggest. Our goal, therefore, is to provide the therapist with suggestions for applying standard treatments to a unique group.

Accordingly, we make certain assumptions about our readers. We assume that our practitioner readers already have a clinical knowledge base, or are in an integrated training program. We will not, therefore, provide extensive clinical background of a generic nature for each problem or disorder. We feel that our contribution is in the *application* of currently received wisdom (such as it is) to our treatment population. Religious professionals who are not clinicians and desire further clinical descriptions, and counselor-educators who require additional material for class presentations, may find this information in our references and suggested readings. We assume that the only motivation necessary to benefit from this book is the desire to be helpful to clergy and religious. We make no assumptions about the reader's personal stance toward religious concerns or even questions of ultimate meaning. We appreciate that many clinicians accept referrals with this population because they are either perceived as having strong religious beliefs by their referral sources, or have an active personal interest in religious concerns and the relationship with personality development.

We feel confident that a sincere desire to help is the only prerequisite for the therapist: First, if our assumption that viewing psychotherapy with religiously committed individuals is correct, then with proper training and motivation the intelligent clinician can stretch to accommodate that group. In theory, effective treatment with clergy by either a lay clinician, or a clinician with no professed religious beliefs, is analogous to a white therapist treating a black client.

Second, research (Propst, Ostrom, Watkins, Dean, & Masburn, 1992) shows that agnostic clinicians were equally as helpful as religious counselors when working with religiously committed depressed persons, *even by helping the clients utilize their specific religious metaphors as a therapeutic aid.*

These assumptions, then, lead us to a final expectation; namely, that as clinicians we are ethically required to understand the cultural context of our clients, to respect that context, and to intervene in ways that do not create cultural ruptures reasonably opposed by the client. We are hopeful that this text will facilitate both that cultural understanding and effective helping of priests, clergy, and vowed religious.

Joseph W. Ciarrocchi
Robert J. Wicks

Terminology

Brother   A male member of a religious community who takes public vows (see *vowed religious*), and is not ordained. Although there are distinctions in Church law between the terms *brothers, monks,* and *friars,* we use the term *brother* in this book to refer to all of these groups generically.

Clergy   An ordained religious minister.

Formation   Term used for the period of training persons for ministry. This is a common term in Roman Catholic circles referring to the training of priests, brothers, monks, and sisters. The phrase *in formation* refers to someone in this training phase.

Minister   Often a term used for ordained persons. We will use it generically to describe those in ministry; e.g., Protestant and Catholic clergy, Catholic sisters, brothers, and deacons.

Seminary   A formation program for ministry in an academic institutional setting, involving a curriculum, generally theological in nature.

Sister   A woman member of a religious community who takes public vows (see *vowed religious*). Although there are technical distinctions in Roman Catholic church law between *sisters* and *nuns,* we use these terms interchangeably in this book.

Vowed Religious   Refers to sisters, nuns, monks, brothers, and priests who are members of religious communities who take public vows such as poverty, chastity (celibacy), and obedience.

Acknowledgments

We want to express our gratitude to those who were supportive of this project. Anna Marie Ciarrocchi and Michaele Wicks provided helpful comments on various drafts of the manuscript. Special thanks to Susan Cooperstein, reference librarian for Loyola College in Maryland, and all the library staff for their wonderful generosity and helpfulness. Will Aycock performed many tasks ably as our graduate assistant. Reverend Jerry Martin and his daughter Lisa Ciarrocchi provided us with valuable insights into the joys and challenges of family life in a minister's home.

We thank Loyola Press for permission to reprint material from *Self-Ministry through Self-Understanding,* and Paulist Press for material from *Handbook of Spirituality for Ministers; The Doubting Disease: Help for Scrupulosity and Religious Obsessions;* and from *Why Are You Worrying?*

PART I

Practical Religious–Cultural Issues

In this brief section two subjects will be discussed as they appear in a unique way among religious professionals: stress and interpersonal relations. As was mentioned in the introduction, information generally found in counseling and psychotherapy primers will, for the most part, not be emphasized. Rather, an effort will be made instead to sensitize counselors and therapists to issues and realities they may encounter in the treatment of ministers within the mainline Christian denominations; namely, priests, Protestant clergy, and Catholic vowed religious (those persons referred to as religious sisters—also commonly referred to as nuns—and religious brothers in this denomination).

1.

Stress

Modern ministry today is dangerous for people who are willing to take leadership roles in organized religion. Chronic and acute secondary stress is high today among Catholic and Protestant clergy, nuns, brothers, and deacons, and it leads many of them into therapy looking for help.

It is fortunate when they avail themselves of this assistance because therapists now have access to a great deal of information on stress reduction. Accordingly, therapists can help full-time ministers to recognize, break down, avoid, and cope with stress in very constructive and effective ways.

However, to provide the best interventions in the area of stress reduction, it is helpful to be sensitive to the form, types, and prevalent causes of pressures that ministry personnel must deal with in their work and life-styles. There are some similarities with others in the helping professions, but given the unique focus and culture of the religious professional's vocation, there are some differences in emphasis and philosophy which particularly affect the dynamics of stress as it is experienced by this group.

CHRONIC SECONDARY STRESS

Much has been made in recent years of the holes in the safety net for the poorest of the poor. We need to face this issue directly because there is a massive discrepancy between the poor and the affluent in our society. Not enough has been said and done about the stress put on the helping professions, especially those in ministry, by having to deal with increasing numbers of those living in poverty. If we don't address the situation, it will further compound the problems being experienced by the needy who depend for support on caring professionals such as Catholic and Protestant clergy, nuns, brothers, and deacons.

In the past 10 years, time and again the authors have seen the brokenness and pain of those who have spent their lives reaching out to others in need. Often such a client has asked for our help, simply because they "cared too much." In the process of helping others they had gotten so involved that their "psychological fingers" were burned. As a result, they have lost perspective, their emotional hearts are tired, and some of them even deeply question their faith commitment.

The reality is that needy people come to those in ministry with basic physical needs, emotional hunger, and spiritual disillusionment. They often present overwhelming problems which have no ready solutions and ask spiritual questions about why God permits suffering (theodicy) that can't be answered with ready formulas.

Today there is decreasing status for those in ministry to fall back upon for security in the face of such all-encompassing need. Such issues as pedophilia, the hypocrisy of some well-known evangelists, and a general tendency to project unfairly onto people in ministry, has led to the latter being persons subject to public scorn and negative transference. These are reactions they neither expect nor deserve, having often given up so much to serve others.

So, what can be done to help those people remain committed who wish to answer the call to enter or remain in ministry? How can they extend their emotional flame to others without being burned out in the process?

Although there are many answers (all incomplete of course) to these two overarching questions, there are three logical steps in helping those in ministry deal with chronic stress (or what has long been referred to in the literature as "burnout" or "compassion fatigue"): (1) recognizing who are ideal candidates for burnout; (2) being sensitive to the major causes of undue prolonged stress in clergy and religious; and (3) knowing some basic preventive steps to lessen the amount and duration of unnecessary stress in their lives.

IDEAL CANDIDATES FOR BURNOUT

Although ministry, as in the case of other helping professions, sets up all those in the field for burnout, there are some who are more apt than others to fall prey to the destructive elements of chronic stress. Knowing a general profile of these vulnerable types helps one make a more speedy informal diagnosis. In addition, it helps to formulate a way to share this information with the minister. This is important because just as in the case of posttraumatic stress disorder (PTSD), people are on the road to improvement when they begin to see an outline of the syndrome they are experiencing; appreciate that others are also in the same category (so they can see their responses are understandable); and can have cause for hope since this issue is not new to the therapist and interventions have been made in the past to deal with it.

For our purposes here, and to further clarify our position, two types of ideal candidate for burnout will be described: the undisciplined ministerial activist and the nonassertive ("chronically nice") minister.

Undisciplined ministerial activists represent a key group of religious professionals who are prime candidates for burnout. A priest once referred to those Jesuits (the informal name for the Society of Jesus, a Roman Catholic order of religious brothers and priests) who were involved in intense social ministry as being almost certain eventual victims of burnout. He quipped that they had a longevity in their work equal to that of members of a bomb squad!

On the surface this pattern may seem surprising because of Christianity's theoretical emphasis on "grace," the action of God in the world. For instance, St. Ignatius Loyola, the founder of the Jesuits, noted that his men should act as if everything were in their hands while appreciating that in reality everything is in God's hands. This emphasis on grace is also present in Protestant teaching, if not more so.

According to this doctrine then, theoretically the minister should be "burnout resistant" since he or she believes God is involved in doing all the heavy work. However, even though among both Roman Catholics and Protestants there is a stated emphasis on God having the key role in producing results (what some Protestants would term *sola fide*, being saved by faith alone), in reality, the major emphasis is on "works" (what the individual can do to change the situation) and only lip service is paid to faith. So, rather than the person in ministry working hard but then being able to gain distance from the need for results because of a deep faith that God will provide, albeit in a mysterious way, this attitude is generally absent for the most part among professional ministers.

And so, when stress does occur and the minister asks for help, the therapist can help those in ministry by using the same therapeutic guidelines as with other patient populations. For instance, the person can be helped to break down situations into ones which they either can or cannot do something about. The patients can be helped through cognition to see the difference between concern about a problem which leads them to do something constructive, and preoccupation with a problem which only leads to destructive and debilitating rumination.

In the case of persons of belief, the culture of religion in which they operate can also be employed as an aid. An overinvolved Catholic nun, who was a workaholic, spurred on by anxiety that she was not doing enough, presents a classic example of this possibility.

She was being seen by a psychologist in his office in a Catholic college. After she presented her dilemma, the psychologist looked at her, pointed up at one of the crucifixes that the college had hung in all the classrooms and offices, and said: "I can hear all of the good work you are doing. Now, what about his role in all that you do? How do you allow for that on a day-to-day basis given your religious beliefs?''

This simple action on the therapist's part was enough to break through her initial resistance to seeing her attitude toward ministry in a different way. He then went on to help her formulate in her own culturally syntonic faith dimension how to prevent undisciplined overinvolvement by using a reality therapy framework with an added faith dimension to reinforce it. When confronted with poverty and overwhelming injustices, this sister felt impelled to react in an unbridled way because of the great need she saw, and personal guilt she felt. In response the psychologist offered her this simple structured outline:

Recognize the givens (The extent and type of specific problem);
Understand the givens (What plans can be made to intervene given the resources available);
Embrace the givens (Do what you can do);
Live within the givens (Know you are limited and after you have done what you can, based on your own faith perspective, let God take care of the residue).

Another ideal candidate for burnout is the nonassertive person who is constantly involved in an intense helping role. Today, given the demands of the greater society and religious society in particular, which includes parishes, religious schools, and other types of religious institutions, there is a prevalent feeling that taking time off is a luxury. Paradoxically, when a person fails to take time off, frequently he or she leaves the field temporarily (hospitalization) or permanently through a change in vocation.

Protestant and Catholic clergy in busy parishes may easily fall prey to involving themselves in long hours of work with no boundaries in place to help them set limits. The environmental reasons for this are present in practically every parish. If we add to this mix someone whose self-esteem is driven by public opinion and who tries to model Christ by being "chronically nice" (when even a cursory reading of the New Testament demonstrates that Jesus was *not* on many occasions), and we have a person who:

Has a hard time setting limits with others or structuring time, even when the parish is a very large one with numerous evening meetings (which as any pastor will tell you is a large drain on his or her energy);

Is very sensitive to criticism no matter who the source is or how invalid the comment;

Tries to meet the demands of a diverse population of people with no sense of nuance as to what can and should be accomplished with each group;

Does not value personal time and places time with family in the same category as leisure;

Does not see the value of modeling assertive, self-caring behavior for the congregation. Instead, the person embraces the "martyr role" and all of the secondary gain it provides. This leads to "going the extra mile" all the time without discriminating between when this should or should not be done;

Has problems in interacting with people when they are angry and ruminates about situations with parishioners and colleagues which didn't result in an easy exchange in which people left happy; and

Is concerned about "numbers": number of new parishioners; how many people attend church services or events; how many people thank him or her after a homily; how much money is donated each week; and how many meetings he or she has attended.

This type of person, whom the authors label as *chronically nice*, is a sure candidate for burnout, and enters treatment in most instances with the proclamation that: "This overwhelming situation has just got to stop!" However, as in the case of therapy patients in general, the real request being made is for relief or a cure in which they do *not* have to change their belief system or behavior but somehow magically can feel better in spite of it all.

To them assertiveness equals aggression, for which they surely will pay. The only time they feel they can express negativity is when they have been martyred long enough and have enough proof to show they may have a right to express anger.

When this occurs, the religious professional is no different from the general population. The outburst of anger is usually non-productive, though admittedly somewhat cathartic, and at some level enjoyable and thus self-reinforcing.

Although scheduling, stress-management skills, and communication techniques are helpful, it is their belief system or personality style, transference, and the presence of an archaic superego, that plagues these individuals. No matter where they work or with whom they interact they are too much concerned about what people think of them.

Therefore, with this type of person, depending on the therapeutic approaches being employed, attention must be given to their style of belief, with all the erroneous elements that are contained in it that have not as yet been fully realized, explored, and challenged. In addition, the archaic superego and unconscious must be confronted along with these clients' extreme fear of rejection of limits under the religious rubric of: "Going the extra mile." This is imperative because when someone cannot discriminate between the crosses they are being called by God to carry and those which they inflict upon themselves, the result is burnout and the inability to carry any crosses at all.

MAJOR CAUSES OF MINISTERIAL BURNOUT

There are many factors about which the therapist should be aware that are major contributors to ministerial burnout. These include: failure to discern what tasks-problems ("crosses") they must take on and which can be set aside; a seamless work schedule; sexism; and anticlericalism. In addition, there are naturally a number of other causes we should note as well (see Table 1.1)

DISCERNMENT OF "CROSSES"

Among the chief problems for those in ministry is not knowing when to say "No." Part of the problem is a failure to appreciate when they should or should not follow the biblical injunction to "go the extra mile."

TABLE 1.1
Causes of Burnout

1. Inadequate quiet time ("prayer"), physical rest, cultural diversion, further education, and personal psychological replenishment.
2. Vague criteria for success or inadequate positive feedback on efforts made.
3. Guilt over failures, and over taking out time to nurture oneself properly to deal with one's own legitimate needs.
4. Unrealistic ideals that are threatening rather than generally motivating.
5. Inability to deal with anger.
6. Extreme need to be liked by others, prompting unrealistic involvement with others.
7. Neglect of emotional, physical, and spiritual needs.
8. Poor community life or unrealistic expectations and needs surrounding the support and love of others for us.
9. Working with people (peers, superiors, those coming for help) who are burned out.
10. Extreme lack of power to effect needed change or being overwhelmed by paperwork and administrative tasks.
11. A serious lack of appreciation by superiors, colleagues, or those whom we are trying to serve.
12. Sexism, agism, racism, or other prejudice experienced directly in life and work.
13. High conflict in the family, home, work, or living environment.
14. A serious lack of charity among those with whom we must live or work.
15. Extreme change during times in life when maturational crises and adjustments are also occurring (for example, a 48-year-old female nun who is being asked to work with difficult adolescents at a time when she is experiencing conflict in her own life).
16. Seeing money wasted on projects that seem to have no relation to helping people or Christian activism.
17. Not having the freedom or power to deal with or absent oneself from regularly occurring stressful events.
18. A failure to curb one's immature reasons for helping others and to develop more mature ones in the process.
19. The "savior complex," an inability to recognize what we can and cannot do in helping others in need.
20. Overstimulation or isolation and alienation.

Source: From *Self-Ministry through Self-Understanding,* edited by R. Wicks (pp. 88, 89). Copyright © 1990 by R. Wicks. Reprinted by permission of Loyola Press.

One of the ways the authors have tried to help those in ministry in this regard is to enter their biblical framework. In the Scriptures, to discern whether something is good or bad, there is an emphasis on addressing the question: "What are the fruits?" If the fruits (results) are bad, then it is not something good; if they are good, then even if on the surface it might not seem desirable, it may well be in the eyes of God.

In working with this population, the psychological implications of answering this question fall into two categories: (1) Does carrying this cross (responding to this person, request, need . . .) produce anxiety, depression, and undue stress? (2) Does embracing this cross produce challenge, peace, or satisfaction—even when responding may be exhausting or quite emotionally taxing?

If the answer to the first question is yes, the minister has to look at whether the "call" he or she perceives from God to go the extra mile in this instance is really the result of personal compulsion rather than the desire to be helpful. If the answer is yes to the second question, then the person knows that this particular crisis was one they really needed to respond to in this instance.

Following this train of thought, a good discussion can be held with persons in ministry about the need to take care of themselves both psychologically and spiritually. Then, metaphorically their emotional arms can be free to carry crosses when they are presented and discerned to be the right ones to shoulder. What persons in ministry must learn is what therapists have been taught for years; namely, that if balance, distance, a sense of one's own limits, and an appreciation of the absolute need for rest, good food, exercise, and leisure are not present, then burnout is not a potential danger, it is a certainty!

A SEAMLESS WORK SCHEDULE

More and more in today's stress-prone world the line between work and personal time has become blurred; nowhere is this more evident than for religious professionals.

Protestant ministers who seek therapy often list among their chief complaints a work "day" that starts early and often ends late in the night. People expect to see them during the day, as with other professions, but also are surprised when they don't attend meetings in the evening, *every* meeting. Moreover, even when the minister is present on Saturday and Sunday, there is often a sense of surprise when a day is taken off during the week, or the minister doesn't come in until 1:00 p.m. on a day when he or she may be busy at the church until the late evening.

This work-related stress frequently causes problems in the minister's family life because of their physical and emotional unavailability. Female spouses will bear the burden of receiving calls for the pastor and be responsible for raising the children almost singlehandedly. In addition, when the spouse who has been involved in ministry all day returns home, he or she is often exhausted emotionally as well as physically and it can be hard to shift gears and be available to the spouse as an equal or present to the children as a parent.

Women ministers describe additional stressors that relate to both generic expectations of women's role in our culture and the specific expectations of their religious group. The married woman pastor, like her lay counterpart, on average will do the majority of the housework and childrearing. She will not generally have the material or emotional support available to men who juggle work and family life. Furthermore, the expectations that she integrate her ministry and family life successfully are strong in that family stability is a universal religious ideal. How often women clergy make the tongue-in-cheek comment of how much they need a wife!

To help a minister with these stresses, a number of interventions normally employed by the therapist will be useful. In addition, a simple stress-reduction suggestion such as taking a short period of time (15 to 45 minutes) to quiet down, take a walk, listen to some music, or pray alone in the church before returning home, sometimes can have a markedly beneficial impact. It can be a wind-down time for the person to get in touch with emotions, release them, and cognitively shift gears before running home into another situation with its own unique sets of rewards and demands.

Phone calls at home, often a parish house provided by the church, are not seen as unusual, neither are visits to the parish house in cases of perceived as well as real emergencies. (We will discuss the unique stresses of this fishbowl existence on ministers and their families in chapter 2.)

A Catholic priest, whose rectory is also his home, will experience this lack of distance. As a result, if on his Thursday off, the priest decides to stay home to do a few personal chores, he may have to deal with parishioner or staff resentment if he ignores doorbells and the telephone.

Nuns also are not exempt either from being drawn into a schedule where work never ends. This is especially the case during times of family need or crisis where the sister is expected to serve as primary helper to a sick mother or troubled sibling as well as hold down a full-time ministerial position and be wholeheartedly present to her religious community.

Nuns work in a remarkable range of settings. Traditionally, they taught in or were administrators in religious schools ranging from preschool to universities. Many also worked in health care as nurses, physicians, or hospital administrators. They carried this work to developing countries, often risking their own health and safety. Today there is no area of service unknown to nuns. They administer homeless shelters, women's advocacy services, AIDS programs, orphanages, and nursing homes, as well as their traditional educational and hospital-based service. Their roles include physician, nurse, psychologist, social worker, professional counselor, educator, theologian, administrator, and attorney, to name but a few. Their achievements are as notable at the corporate level as at the personal level. They have created model schools run with an economic efficiency that is the envy of taxpayers who unfavorably compare their expensive public school counterparts. Nuns' communities have corporately structured several of the most respected and financially well-managed hospital chains in the United States, which also remain sensitive to the health care needs of the poor. Given their shrinking numbers, the increasing burden of caring for their own community's aging population, and a desire to maintain their current ministry commitments, the stress of multiple roles for these women defies quantification. When one's own family issues are added to the mix, as the following case illustrates, the pressure is overwhelming.

One sister, a religion teacher and superior of her convent, described her situation as a never-ending pull in 12 different directions. She was expected to be prepared for class and provide leadership for her convent. Yet, her family gave her the message that since she wasn't married, she should be home anytime her mother needed her.

Although she would complain about their attitude and the demands on her, she would often drop everything she was doing (which would cause guilt) so that she could respond to any problem concerning her mother. Also, every weekend she would go home to attend to her mother who she felt might die in the near future.

Treatment was based on having her look at the belief systems that were driving this behavior. The following is a sampling of some of those belief systems, and how, whenever possible, in addressing them, religious values espoused by the sister were capitalized on so that the intervention was culturally based:

> The patient needed to see that her mother might well die when she was at school. Once this reality was accepted, she was asked to formulate a plan that included spending one weekend each month away from the convent and her mother, visiting with a friend. She was then asked to look at her daily schedule and write it up in detail so it could be reviewed in treatment. (One thing that came out of this discussion was a more balanced approach to her work as a teacher. She came to see that after 32 years as a teacher, it was not unreasonable for her to ask for an assignment that dealt strictly with adults and was less demanding than working 8 hours a day with adolescents.)

> "Love your neighbor as yourself" was introduced so the sister could examine whether in fact she did love herself. This was done to help her see the difference between love that is unconditional and derives from a healthy perspective, and compulsive love driven by an archaic superego and overconcern with one's image. It also helped her realize that by modeling self-love, she was in fact indirectly empowering other nuns as well as women in general. (This led to a discussion on sexism which also allowed her to express anger for the first time about the patriarchal structure of her church. This opportunity to recognize, share, and process feelings is obviously also an aid to stress reduction and a motivator for personal autonomy.)

Examination of the seamless work schedule so common to those in ministry, can lead to a schedule reorientation and thus to stress reduction. Furthermore, as can be seen in the sketch of the above case, it can also lead to possibilities in personal growth, an appreciation of one's own needs, more assertive behavior, and greater self-esteem.

SEXISM

For the female Protestant pastor, the scenario in which the chronically nice behavior described above seems to be almost a requirement for success, is unfortunately all too common. Within the past several decades, women have been ordained in most of the mainline Protestant denominations, while the Christian Orthodox, Roman Catholic, and some Baptist denominations have continued to deny them entry into this form of ministry.

On the surface the denominations that ordain both men and women look quite open and egalitarian, and to some degree this is true. However, in most cases, the structure and ethos of the denomination has not changed; it is still a male-oriented, power-based structure. So, while the situation is better in many ways for women in those religious denominations where they can be ordained, in subtle ways it is still destructive. It is especially destructive for the chronically nice woman who feels succeeding on behalf of herself and other women is a must no matter what the sacrifice.

The situation is also very difficult for women who are assertive. When women speak up in the church they are sometimes cast as extreme, angry, aggressive feminists, while similar behavior in men is described in positive terms. The situation is made even worse when women in the congregation and other women ministers identify with the aggressor and support the status quo.

Pastoral relationships are made even more complicated and stressful when the woman in professional ministry (be she a Protestant pastor/associate pastor or Catholic nun) is in the midst of her own growth process and is dealing with males who don't know how to handle anger.

Passive individuals often pass through aggressive stages on the road to finding the balance we refer to as assertiveness. This is a natural process and nothing to be concerned about unless the response received is one that is rejecting, passive-aggressive, or aggressive on the part of a male coworker or superior who has power. The results of this are not only stress for the woman involved but also for the male who is not able to handle angry responses from others.

In such instances, it has been found useful to follow either an individual approach or one in which both people are seen for one or two sessions and taught communication skills and a greater understanding of the dynamics involved. Interpersonal relations often involve many elements which impact communication between ministers themselves and between them and those they serve in the parish (this will be addressed in a subsequent chapter). One of these that deserves a brief mention here in the stress chapter is anticlericalism.

ANTICLERICALISM

In years past, Protestant and Catholic pastors, nuns, brothers, and deacons all had special status in their communities. They received deference and were often accorded a place of honor. Although this is sometimes the case today, the general rule is that not only do they not receive special positive treatment, they also are the recipients of negative transferences which can be the source of a great deal of stress.

One minister said that if he were asked what he would like from those he served it would be that they would treat him with the same expectations they had for others, then he could live more humanly without looking over his shoulder as to what people were saying about him. In another instance a Catholic priest was doing a census of his parish and he knocked at the wrong door when looking for a particular parishioner. The response from behind the closed door was: "Go away. We don't have any small boys in here for you Father."

Helping clergy deal with the negative transference issues more prevalent in society today is an essential part of any stress reduction treatment. It is easy for a cleric to take personally the negative comments aimed at him or her and to try to live up to the impossible positive transference. The therapist can focus very profitably on this area because it will open up a full discussion of such important questions as: Why did I become a minister or priest? Why do I stay in this role now? How do I feel about myself, and what are the comments which quickly change these feelings? How do I react when I feel I am being unfairly viewed by others?

Still, the fact that negative transference does exist is problematic for those in ministry today and, though it is not pleasant, it need not be awful. As a matter of fact, as with all problems, there are positive aspects. One is that without status, there is no need to worry about secondary gain. Pastoral work can be undertaken because it is what the person in ministry wants to do based on his or her belief system.

The Dalai Lama told Thomas Merton, a Catholic priest, during a brief meeting in India, a story which is related to such positive possibilities. When the Chinese were becoming more restrictive in Tibet, a Rimpoche wrote to the Dalai Lama: "Do we stay or do we leave?" The Dalai Lama's reply: "Well, now brother everyone stands on their own two feet."

Father Merton took this comment to translate into: "Well now everyone stands on their faith." To him it meant that structures and status were in flux, and that to be in ministry one had to look deep within oneself and see the mature, lasting reasons for remaining and keeping up "the good fight." Not a bad way to discriminate between reasons that are sound and those tied to unconscious wishes or a belief system filled with erroneous beliefs.

PREVENTION OF BURNOUT
AND "COMPASSION FATIGUE"

The usual repertoire of stress prevention and reduction methods with which the therapist is already familiar will not be reviewed here. However, if therapists can be aware of how some professionals in the field who are aware of the religious culture approach clients who are in ministry, they may be able to borrow from this material according to their own level of comfort and adapt it according to their own therapeutic theory and personal style.

Two specific approaches that have been helpful clinically to the authors are to involve the patients in self-talk and self-questioning which will help them to recognize, dispute, and replace beliefs and thoughts which are dysfunctional (i.e., ones that serve to increase the burnout triad: stress, anxiety, depression).

Accordingly, in Tables 1.2 and 1.3, general information is provided for use with patients or as a guide to help therapists prepare their own handouts for those in ministry. (If the tables, or an adaptation of them, are used as handouts, time taken during the sessions to process the client's reactions to the self-talk in Table 1.2 and initial responses to the questions in Table 1.3 can be quite productive. This can make it easier to diagnose additional or more specific difficulties as well as indicating types of resistance to intervention, including simple misunderstandings regarding homework the therapist may provide.)

Other prevention approaches to common stressors among clergy and religious can be developed according to their individual needs or inability to guide their lives in a healthy way. One way of doing this is by having the client review and then respond in written form to the following statements and questions so they can be discussed in a later session:

1. Persons in ministry often have many responsibilities. Which ones are especially stressful for you? Why do you think that is so? How do you prepare for them? What do you do to process or decompress from them after they are over? How effective is your preparation and aftercare?

2. Pacing in ministry is difficult because each day there are unexpected demands and schedule changes. Given this reality, what can be done to provide greater balance for yourself in ministry?

3. Although ministry is seen as helping people care for their souls, in reality it is often filled with paperwork, finances, and a lot of sometimes tedious activities and meetings. Since

TABLE 1.2
Self-Talk

The following situations and the appropriate questions following them appropriately illustrate how we can correct our thinking so healthy action in difficult stress-related times can become more possible.

1. *When feeling lost, confused, and in darkness:* Am I taking out time for prayer in silence and solitude and do I have a network of friends (including a spiritual director and/or counselor if necessary) to challenge, support, and inform me?

2. *When feeling overworked, underappreciated, undernourished intellectually, bored, or somehow out of balance:* What is in imbalance in my life that needs attention?

3. *When feeling worthless, inadequate, used, belittled, or in some way lacking in good self-image or self-esteem:* How can I find my true reflection in life? In other words, one that is more in line with that of people who appreciate me?

4. *When feeling overwhelmed by others' anger, depression, anxiety, poverty, sense of conflict, or stress:* How can I assert myself and face these persons and also maintain enough distance so I can continue to walk with them and others in darkness?

5. *When faced with a mistake, loss of image, or failure:* How can I give up my belief that my image is so important and that if I make a mistake (which may cause guilt) I erroneously believe that *I* am a mistake (evidence of shame)? Why is it that I think I can succeed in all cases with all people when this is impossible? (Ideals are good when they inspire us; to feel one must absolutely achieve them is irrational.)

6. *When people don't like us:* Why must I believe that everyone must respect and like me? If it didn't happen to Jesus or any of the great saints, why me?

7. *When we are working very hard in ministry and not succeeding:* What makes me think that if I work as best I can, I will succeed? When Jesus died on the cross he was deemed to be a failure by historians of the day.

8. *When a close friend fails or someone in authority in the church, our community, or parish team lets us down:* Why do I expect that friendships must be perfect? How can I better appreciate the good times in the relationship and realize that the difficulties are worth the learning it offers me for the future?

9. *When people make fun of me or don't take me seriously:* People are never prophets in their own country; how can I better recognize this? (Also, when one moves from a time in the day when one is a "transference figure," such as a minister, to one's position as a peer, friend, or family member, the jolt in the change of role is something that is tough to accept and must be taken into consideration.)

(continued)

TABLE 1.2 (continued)

10. *When we feel as if we aren't very prayerful, don't really know how to pray, or feel like a sinner who doesn't deserve to be in ministry:* What would make one expect that ministry brings with it a special sense of holiness or the ability to be good at prayer? (Thomas Merton [a famous contemplative] often reminded people that with prayer, with God, we are always in over our head. He also acknowledged that on occasion we want to give up, and this is natural, but that we must recognize that courage comes and goes, so we should hold on for the next supply.)

Source: From *Handbook of Spirituality for Ministers*, Vol. 1 edited by R. J. Wicks (pp. 256–258). Copyright © 1995 by Robert J. Wicks. Used by permission of Paulist Press.

this is so, what are the meaningful activities you are involved in and how do you draw energy from them?

4. Even though in theory people of faith should be able to risk more than others because their identity and hopes are based on a belief in God, too often level of comfort is traded for peace, and the result is a life of little risk. What are the reasonable risks you take in your ministry? How do you discriminate between actions that involve reasonable risk and ones in which you are being rash and which may have untoward consequences?

5. In ministry, as in therapy, often the person must keep his or her emotions under wraps so the helping relationship is not sidetracked by the helper's own needs, feelings, or problems (countertransference). Despite this, it is essential for the helper to still be aware of his or her own feelings, thinking, and beliefs, so actions taken are ones which are healthy and productive. How do you stay in touch with your feelings and do you share them each day with a person you trust by meeting with him or her or by talking on the phone?

6. Perfectionism and workaholism are rampant in any of the helping professions, worst of which may be ministry because of its historical concern with rooting out imperfections and an inaccurate interpretation of the biblical injunction to "Be perfect as your Father in heaven is perfect." (This statement means you should try to be truly you as God is truly God; instead it is read that you should be as perfect as God, in other words, be God.) Given this, how patient do you feel you are with yourself and the imperfections in others? When you are

TABLE 1.3
Self-Questioning

Balance

Is this lack of physical and psychospiritual energy and motivation something temporary, or have I set myself up for burnout? What is the value of personal meditation and "holiday hours" (coffee breaks, evenings with friends) in my life?

Has something changed in my life that makes me feel that I need to work so hard that I'm neglecting myself? Am I trying to prove something to someone or to myself?

What kind of positive and negative feedback am I getting from the environment because I'm working so hard? (Are people telling me not to work so hard, but indirectly giving me signs that they expect me to labor continuously?)

Expectations

How much do I expect to be appreciated for what I do?

Do I expect everyone to like and respect me?

Does what I expect of myself turn out to be a source of motivation for me to be the best I can, or a source of personal disappointment? ("I'm not as good as I should be; I'm failing in my vocation.")

Are my expectations of others tied to the reality of the situation or based on my own unresolved needs to be loved? ("Do I serve others so they will like me and tell me how great I am, or primarily because I want to be of service?")

Knowledge

How do I perceive my current work and living situations? Are they supportive? If so, when are they? If not, what is contributing to this?

Do I feel I am making the most of my current situation? How am I doing this and how am I failing in this regard?

When something unpleasant happens, do I analyze the situation to see what part I played in making the situation better or worse?

How do I learn from stress and rejection? (Do I seek to understand myself and others better when things don't go my way to see how I might benefit from such knowledge?)

What are my realistic and immature motivations to help specific people in my life whom I am in the process of supporting emotionally?

Do I really try to be empathic with others so I am not surprised by their expectations and demands of me?

How do I work to continue to develop my knowledge of professional issues in psychology and theology?

(continued)

TABLE 1.3 (continued)

Support

What kinds of people do we seek out as friends and why?

Are we willing to entertain relationships with different types of people?

Are we frightened of being clear with people about our personal feelings because we are afraid to lose them as friends?

When we are angry do we own up to the anger and try to see what is happening in interpersonal encounters to bring it on?

What do we expect of our community, friends, and family? Do we expect too much, or have we failed to become involved with others in our life?

Can we reach out to others when we are feeling down and anxious? Are we constantly complaining and crying to others?

Do we feel that we are a member of a group, or are we becoming more and more alienated from the natural communities of people with whom we should be involved (a spiritual director, a more experienced colleague, etc.)?

Have we found supportive supervisors in our lives who can help us in time of need?

Do we find we can express our feelings clearly and often enough without burdening others or making them feel that it is always their fault we are suffering?

In being honest with others, do we also remember we should be charitable too and get the same type of respect from them?

Source: From *Self-Ministry through Self-Understanding,* edited by R. Wicks (pp. 90–93). Copyright © 1990 by R. Wicks. Reprinted by permission of Loyola Press.

overly critical, how do you catch yourself and recognize this? Once you do recognize it, how do you deal with it?

VICARIOUS POSTTRAUMATIC STRESS/ACUTE SECONDARY STRESS

Unfortunately causes of psychological trauma are not unusual today. Psychotherapists are aware of this on two levels. First, there is an appreciation of an increase in the number of sexual and physical abuse cases, and in parts of the country the presence of new referrals due to natural/human-made disasters. On another level, recently there have been a number of books published on acute secondary stress disorders/vicarious posttraumatic stress. Unlike the burnout literature before it, this material deals with the dangers caused by continual contact with traumatized individuals.

Since those in full-time ministry are often dealing with a population that may demonstrate similar levels of trauma, it is important for therapists to consider acute secondary stress when treating clergy and religious. In addition to the knowledge already possessed on PTSD, which will provide a good basis for interventions, the therapist who works with this population of religious professionals should also be in a position to help those in ministry to be aware of both major (primary) signs of acute secondary stress and common ways (secondary signs) persons suffering from vicarious PTSD may act out inappropriately with their clients or colleagues. In this way, they will be attuned to such behavior in the present and future and be able to seek help for it rather than continue behaving in a way which can cause harm to themselves or others.

Major signs of acute *secondary* stress result when working with survivors of trauma causes a disruption in the helper's view of self and the world. Incest, the violence of rape, child abuse, pedophilia by teachers, scout leaders, and clergy, teenage murder, and the mugging of the elderly are only some of the traumatic events which demonstrate pervasive, often randomly inflicted cruelty, decrease the sense (or illusion) of security, and increase distrust to the paranoid level.

Primary Signs of Stress

1. Doubts about one's power to effect change in any meaningful way in today's cruel, unjust world.
2. A dramatic increase in one's sense of cynicism, lack of trust or faith in the goodness of people's motives.
3. Fears about one's own safety and an increase in one's own sense of vulnerability which may lead to pronounced startle reactions, problems sleeping, nightmares, and a desire to avoid stressful situations or traumatized individuals.
4. Preoccupation with a traumatized person or the trauma the person experienced to the point where it is present constantly in one's discussions, homilies, writings, and dream life.

Secondary Signs of Stress

(Secondary signs are evidenced during interactions with traumatized people):

1. Trying to force traumatized people to "get over it" quickly rather than recognizing recovery as a lifelong process in which a typical initial healing process takes 3 to 5 years. This time-frame includes not only ministerial guidance but professional therapy as well as support by good friends willing to be very available in person and over the phone.
2. Blaming the victim of trauma.
3. Directly or indirectly giving the message to the person that you are unwilling to listen to a recounting of the abuse or other form of trauma he or she experienced.
4. Overinvolvement with a person based on the belief that only you can cure this person, resulting in no limits being set, sexual involvement, and a removal of the right for self-determination by the survivor.
5. Interventions with the survivor (blaming, manipulation, hostility, distancing) based on the erroneous belief that it was not the trauma but personal or spiritual weakness that is the source of current problems.
6. Promising unrealistic personal availability to a client, then withdrawing even reasonable time as a stabilizing force in the individual's life.
7. Providing quick spiritual or biblical "fixes" to the survivor rather than being willing to sit with the person in the dark parts (fear, anxiety, anger, depression, grief) of the journey toward recovery and the point when the trauma can be reintegrated as a healing experience into the person's newly strengthened personality and place in life.
8. An unwillingness to face with the person the reality that certain losses as a result of trauma may not be compensable in the way the person would like them to be.

The important point to make with patients who are in full-time ministry is that the above reactions are natural ones when

one is confronted with overwhelming negative material or behavior. Accordingly, the best approach is to provide information which will aid in prevention of unnecessary secondary
trauma, and increase the ability of the pastor to interact with
parishioners or students who are survivors of trauma. Finally,
there is a need to sensitize the religious professional to the
need to quickly recognize when his or her behavior is inappropriate or when the person is experiencing some level of trauma.

In addition, it is worth noting again that intense transference, in and of itself, whether the person is a survivor of abuse
or not, can be traumatic for the unaware minister. Sharing
information on PTSD with the client can help them appreciate
this reality as well. Moreover, the issue of transference is so
important in terms of the minister's psychological well-being
that it will be a key topic in the next chapter on interpersonal relations.

2.

Interpersonal Relations
and Family Issues

Of all the helping professions, ministry is at its core probably the one which is most interpersonal in nature. Whether the minister is leading the congregation in prayer, meeting one-to-one with a troubled parishioner, or leading a parish council meeting, the bottom line is community and Jesus' words: "Where two or more are gathered in my name, I am there."

Christianity is first and foremost a religion of the interpersonal. This was set culturally in motion by Jesus in his work with the 12 apostles. Even when he was concerned with one of them, he would normally bring the rest of them together before teaching the lesson or challenging their view of the world, both religious and secular.

Protestant and Catholic clergy, nuns, brothers, and deacons know this when they enter the seminary or religious life. Also, in the case of Catholic nuns and brothers, part of the reason they are entering a religious order, society, or congregation is their desire to both live and work with others following the same type of life.

Yet, it is in the interpersonal arena that many professionals in ministry seem to have difficulty and turn to therapy for help. The therapist can deal with many of the presenting complaints by employing standard therapeutic work. But, as in the case of stress, it may be helpful to look at a number of areas which seem specifically to be problems within the ministerial client population. These include: understanding and handling *intense transference, passive-aggressiveness,* and *loneliness.*

INTENSE TRANSFERENCE

As was mentioned in the opening chapter on stress, transference is something which few in ministry are trained to understand or deal with either in a seminary or in an initial religious formation program.

By helping Protestant and Catholic ministers become more sensitive to their feelings (and the thoughts and beliefs that produce them), therapists can help them gain insight into their own reactions. In addition, it can help them become more aware of the parishioners' issues which may have in some way triggered such a response on their part. Some of the major feelings described by ministers in this regard are:

Fear
Erotic feelings
Annoyance/anger
Detachment
Feeling used or manipulated

The *fear* reported by ministers can obviously be attributable to a number of causes. However, more often than not it is precipitated by a parishioner or colleague manifesting some behavior which the minister does not have a planned way to handle. These include:

Depression and suicidal behavior
Extreme pathology such as psychosis, paranoia, or manic–depressive behavior
Aggressive behavior
Extreme overdependence
Sexual transference

In each of the instances, the minister can be helped to become aware of the cause of the behavior and how to handle it through simple interventions, limit-setting, and (when necessary) referral. The fear then becomes a diagnostic aid to his or her pastoral care rather than a debilitating factor.

Erotic feelings are a natural part of working closely with people. They point to the immaturity and unintegrated personality factors in the helper as well as the almost innate physical reaction (e.g., erection in males) we have been conditioned to have in response to certain cues. The minister needs to be aware of such feelings rather than to screen them out or belittle them. In addition, he or she must be helped to see clearly the difference between feelings one has and acting upon such feelings.

The therapist needs to explain to the minister that eroticism can be produced by clients who are hysterical, very needy, and those whose trust has been violated and who wish to have someone in their lives who will care for them but be responsible for boundary-setting. Unfortunately, there are also those sociopathic individuals who wish to manipulate the minister for financial or other gain. (This is especially the case when the minister is homosexual and has not shared this with his or her congregation or religious denomination/order.)

Therapists receive a great deal of education surrounding the need to recognize positive transference of a sexual nature for what it is, *transference*. However, someone who has not received such training and is in a high pressure position may well respond to the transference as if it were reality-based. When this happens in many cases it ends in problems for both parties.

Married ministers often feel the psychological jolt when they move from their (largely transferential) position as a minister to one in which they are just husbands or wives whose spouse is not hanging on every word or suggestion. Also, because the minister may be suffering from some level of burnout or secondary PTSD because of unexamined and unresolved feelings related to constant, intense interactions in the parish, there may be a tendency on the part of the minister to feel misunderstood or unappreciated at home. This may in turn lead the spouse to feel the same when his or her relating of the day's events doesn't seem interesting or important enough. Add someone who comes in for spiritual guidance who is manifesting a sexualized transference, and the stage is set for the minister to act upon an impulse that should be suppressed and instead understood.

Annoyance/anger are also often unnecessary reactions (countertransference) that are triggered by the transference of obsessive-compulsive or borderline personalities who are not recognized by the minister as individuals with long-term ingrained dysfunctional styles of dealing with the world. Thus, the minister personalizes the actions of the parishioner or colleague in question and reacts out of a sense of being treated unfairly or competitively.

By understanding, through the therapy, the dynamics of the interactions as well as being better attuned to the dynamics *within* the persons with whom they must deal, they may be able to increase their effectiveness along with decreasing their loss of energy. Also, they will be able to use their sense of anger as a personal barometer of other issues that are unresolved in themselves around the area of confrontation and assertiveness. (We will discuss this further when addressing the topic of passive aggressiveness.)

Feeling detached is another typical countertransference response on the part of the minister when confronted with certain forms of transference or the presentation of difficult material by a parishioner or colleague. Sexual or physical abuse, cruelty, extreme poverty, racism or sexism, and graphic reports of trauma often lead a helper to react through helplessness, fear, hopelessness, or a personal sense of being overwhelmed or insecure. Such countertransference is compensated for through a sterile form of detachment that is not consciously employed as "keeping a therapeutic distance/limits" can be.

When this isolation of affect takes place, the therapist needs to have the issues being presented so "clinically" by the minister revisited with a sensitivity to any affect that might be present. Focusing on affect by supplying it with a statement such as: "When hearing stories like that many of us really feel a number of things," may also give the person permission to get in touch with feelings that have been kept at bay through extreme detachment.

Feeling used or manipulated is a common complaint of ministers when they come into treatment. With respect to transference, this type of response is to persons who fall into the sociopathic, narcissistic, and borderline diagnostic categories. In a religious setting, these three personality types can wreak havoc, especially for religious superiors who come into therapy because they are at their wits end with certain members of their denomination, congregation, or church.

The problem in these instances is that ministers are educated in such a way that they treat everyone in distress as if they were suffering from an anxiety disorder. Consequently, they approach even the sociopath and borderline with the stance, all I need do is listen, allow the person to open up, and support them in any way I can by giving them a sense of greater freedom and possibility, and they will see that all is well. Unfortunately, this leads to manipulation by both the sociopath and borderline for different dynamic reasons, and winds up disrupting the religious community. In addition, these people take up an inordinate amount of time.

The therapist's role in helping the minister cope with these types of individuals is to enable them to see that it is essential for good pastoral care to understand which people fall into which category. Just as the surgeon who gave an appendectomy to everyone who was referred would have uneven surgical results, so too the minister must recognize that a pastoral diagnosis is important for proper ministry to others.

And so it is essential to help those in ministry to understand the concept of transference. Once they see and understand it better, they will be able to understand people's actions more clearly and will be better able to avoid falling into the trap of acting upon both the negative and positive transference they receive. In addition, they will be able to start noting their own countertransference toward people. This will enable them to pick up styles of behavior that don't fit the situation or persons and will allow them to adjust their expectations accordingly.

PASSIVE AGGRESSIVENESS[1]

Organized religion typically is an "ideal environment" for the development and nurturing of passive aggressiveness. The constant smiles of some religious cult members are really only mild caricatures of the sweet veneers that many people in ministry must wear if they are to consider themselves true followers of the Gospel.

Those in ministry and the social unit within which they operate (i.e., church, religious community, Christian school) are often dynamically loyal to a style which praises control, suppression, repression, denial of anger, and avoidance of conflict. As one might expect, the results of such a psychological philosophy of living can easily lead to personal devastation, an apathetic community, or involvement in "religious" causes that are based on legalism or extremism, serving to unconsciously deliver hostility instead of the "Good News" of the Gospel which ministers say they wish to present to others. For example, some individuals concerned with doctrinal orthodoxy write critiques of opponents that include quotations out of context, misquotes, personal attacks, and, at times, outright calumny, all in the name of advancing religious purity.

When anger is not recognized and channeled constructively in a minister or religious community or institution, a lack of growth, or increase in personal or communal pathology is the expected outcome. Illustrations of this, unfortunately, are easy to uncover. The following are four obvious ones:

> The accommodating minister who gets along with *everyone* in the parish but develops an ulcer, hypertension, or problems with alcoholism or obesity in the process.

> The nice, but insular and stagnant Christian church or school that is so fearful of anger being experienced in its midst that it discourages and denies conflict in any form.

---

[1] Part of this material is an adaptation of R. Wicks (1983). Passive-aggressiveness within the religious setting. In R. Parsons & R. Wicks (Eds.), *Passive aggressiveness: Theory and practice* (pp. 213–227). New York: Brunner/Mazel.

The Catholic sister who does everything by the letter of the law and devotes much of her energy to keeping from breaking it herself and to ensuring others don't venture out of its bounds as well.

The Christian activist (e.g., for peace, antiabortion) who acts with such a vengeance that his or her message defeats the purported Christian one the activist claims to be delivering to others by witnessing the truth.

The fact that there are abundant illustrations of people in ministry who are not in touch with their anger, much less aware of their ability and need to use it constructively, can be traced to the traditional misunderstandings that Christians have had with regard to anger.

CHRISTIAN CONFUSION ABOUT ANGER

Perfection as a goal can be inspirational. Yet, when it has as one of its tenets the elimination of anger as an emotion, it is a threatening, misguided norm for Christians to follow. Taking New Testament injunctions out of context is probably one of the key determinants of confusion or distortion which leads Christians to want to avoid anger at all costs.

Jesus' admonition to "turn the other cheek" and Paul the Apostle's encouragement to "put off the old nature" have long been consciously and indirectly employed as supports for the need to subdue one's anger. However, to interpret Christ and Paul in this way is to assume that loving one's neighbor and reviewing–renewing one's life in Christ is tantamount to denying one's own God-given human nature, which includes emotions such as anger. Ministers seeking and preaching such perfection need to see that they are also making light of, or denying, Christ's own displays of anger at the injustices he saw.

As one theologian points out in his very popular book on American spirituality, such an outlook can lead to the removal of justified anger from the center of the Christian's prayer life, which in turn can make life in faith a compartmentalized, artificial one. Sharing the following information with a person in ministry can open up a discussion in the therapy which can prove very useful:

> Piety and social intransigence go to church regularly hand in hand. In this way, love of neighbor is confused with "being nice" (anger, one's very capacity for moral outrage, is a sin) and questions of justice are conveniently considered outside the realm of one's prayer life. In contrast, we have seen that the only real "answer" to prayer is a changed person on the one hand and a changed people, that is a changed world or culture, on the other. (Fox, 1972, pp. 100–101)

Augsburger, a Mennonite on the faculty at Fuller Theological Seminary in California, and the author of *Anger and Assertiveness in Pastoral Care* (1979), also points to the confusion Christian leaders in particular may have when distinguishing between inappropriate "niceness" on the one hand and being a good pastor to those whom he or she is trying to serve on the other. The results of such "niceness" can be quite negative. In his words:

> Chronic niceness in a pastor tends to elicit comparable niceness in others, with the result that the negative feelings are not readily shared and resentments accumulate. . . .
> Habitual niceness inhibits the free expression of natural responses. It prohibits easy discussion of differences, making it hard to initiate frank interchange. Participants are kept on guard by the fear that their relationship could not survive a spontaneous hassle if one should erupt.
> Professional niceness maintains distance between persons. . . . Irritations are handled with a "soft touch" and the more intimate levels of trust and risk go unexplored. . . .
> Perpetual niceness creates patterns of denial in relationships, and the pastor's denying style can help set the tone for a whole community's "united front" method of suppressing conflict. . . . (p. 8)

From the above comments by two theologians, the problems with passive aggressiveness among religious individuals are obviously coming to light and being discussed at last. Moreover, such recognition that anger is a part of full religious living, as well as something that is part of the natural order, means that it can't be as easily dismissed as something inherently "secular" or irrelevant for believing Christians and their ministers as it was in the past.

Even in the case of passive aggressiveness, the issue of misplaced and poorly dealt with anger in religious groups is coming to light, as can be seen in the following quote from *Inside Christian Community* (Hammett and Sofield, 1981):

> Passive–aggressive persons are extremely difficult to deal with because conflict never surfaces and they are unwilling to cooperate. They manage to maintain a rather serene picture of themselves as well-controlled, proper, nonviolent human beings. But they are not the peaceful or loving personalities they pretend to be. When they are confronted with the disruptive nature of their style, they do not easily give up. Often they remain remote and inaccessible to healthy relationships. If any relationship begins to build, the passive–aggressive person quietly withdraws, leaving hurt behind. Unfortunately, this personality is common in religious communities. (p. 75)

Consequently, no longer is the bittersweet veneer of passive–aggressiveness seen as the religious ideal to be followed and modeled. Christian writers and lecturers over the past 15 years have been openly condemning of such pseudolove of neighbor, and these writings and tenets can be used by the therapist in the treatment setting with ministers.

And so, because of changing attitudes, mental health consultants and therapists can now deal with anger-related problems in religious organizations and individuals without undue concern that their interventions will be generally dismissed on theological grounds. In fact, for the past 20 years, pastoral theologians from the larger Christian denominations have been supporting appropriate assertiveness as a way to deal with anger constructively (Augsburger, 1979; Burwicki, 1981; Mickey & Gamble, 1978).

Theories about passive aggressiveness and indirect expression of anger, as well as concomitant methods of intervention based on these therapeutic modalities, are already covered in the literature (Parsons & Wicks, 1983). Knowledge of this material is obviously a first step in preparing for analysis, diagnosis, and strategy for intervention with a patient who is in ministry and is having a problem with understanding and handling the emotion of anger. However, prior to an intervention, it might be helpful for the therapist to review the following material on *recognition of passive aggressiveness and modeling assertiveness: combining the understanding of anger with the practice of ministerial assertiveness.*

RECOGNIZING PASSIVE AGGRESSIVENESS

Appreciating when and how passive aggressiveness is present is the logical place to start in presenting an overview of this style of indirectly dealing with anger. In the Christian setting, though by no means restricted to it, there are a number of "classic ways" in which persons demonstrate passive aggressiveness. In working with ministers, noting such illustrative ways anger seeps out can be a helpful beginning. Corrective instructions, memos, and training others to avoid anger might be good examples to begin with here. Naturally, there are many more illustrations, but this should serve to give the reader a basic sense of some of the cultural manifestations of this behavior.

Preachers, local religious superiors of Catholic orders or societies, and "prophetic colleagues" who wish to "help" their fellow seminarians, ministers, etc., stay on the right path can use opportunities for corrective *instruction* as times for corrective *destruction*. Illustrations of this are not as few as one would hope. As can be seen in the illustrations, rank or position in the community has no bearing on the opportunity for or presence of passive aggressiveness.

> A priest who becomes angry at dinner hosts who try to force him to drink more than two glasses of wine may not deal directly with his anger at them; instead, he may make a general issue "for the good of the whole parish" and preach on this type of situation on Sunday.

> A minister who has difficulty working with his associate pastor may spend a good deal of time each day telling her what faults she has. Naturally, this is all for her own good so she doesn't continue making the same mistakes.

A seminarian who drops hints for his roommate to be more orderly, based on the assumption that there is some value to doing this indirectly rather than discussing his annoyance more directly, may be quietly trying to drive the other person up the wall (without apparently being un-Christ-like, heaven forbid!)

Writing *memos* is also a popular way for persons in ministry to be passive aggressive or indirectly angry at another person; the technique is well used because it allows the barb to be sent from a distance. Consequently, in a Catholic religious community such written communications are frequently employed to safely censure someone else. A superior may write a note to a member of the community to inform him or her of problems that have come to the superior's attention via another member of the community. A community member may take similar steps. In response to a verbal request to undertake some undesirable task, he or she may respond vaguely or critically in writing to the request rather than dealing with the potential disagreement directly with the superior.

Another familiar memo technique is to leave a message posted regarding something that has produced anger. The memo usually has three elements: (1) justification of one's own stand (as being correct and "Christian"); (2) reference to the injury being caused by other(s) who are vaguely recognizable from the information given; and (3) "pseudoforgiveness" of the person(s) who did it (so he/she/they shouldn't retaliate by being angry). The following is an example of a note that might well be seen on a convent refrigerator:

Signing out the car is something which I feel I have a responsibility to do; consequently, I try to do this well in advance so as not to cause anyone any inconvenience. Yesterday, I wanted to use the car for my usual weekly visit to help my parents and the car was gone. It had been signed out at the last moment to deliver some goods. Though this possibly could have waited, and though I understand that it was a worthwhile trip and I recognize I must also compromise, I do ask that we try to set up these journeys in advance in the future so we don't cause unnecessary hardship to each other.

Thank you.

Too often the problem of passive aggressiveness also continues because ministers *train one another to avoid anger.* Meetings are ideal places for this to occur. If the dynamics are not understood, then healthy persons who are trying to be aware of and constructively deal with anger can be coopted into seeing their own process, rather than a distorted religious one, as inappropriate.

Pastor Smith: Jim you really seemed to be upset at our elders' meeting yesterday.
Jim (Youth Minister): Yes. The way Bill and Mary were trying to close out options other than their own in dealing with the youth group infuriated me. I wanted to let them know, so we could openly deal with it.
Pastor Smith: This is a Christian group, Jim. We all have differences, but anger isn't going to help; you ought to think about controlling it a bit better. We can always drop hints to them when we see them alone.

Rather than encouraging Jim to learn how to channel anger openly in a way that would not be destructive to others, he is encouraging him to suppress it. Only resentment and hidden agendas will result from this action. Also, if it is dealt with as he suggests, the community will never deal with their fears of conflict. Thus, they will never achieve the intimacy needed to become a cohesive group or paradoxically, in religious terms, a "faith community."

MODELING ASSERTIVENESS:
COMBINING THE UNDERSTANDING OF ANGER
WITH THE PRACTICE OF MINISTERIAL ASSERTIVENESS

Once ministers stop seeing the emotion of anger as being either good or bad and recognize it as a sign of their own personal vitality, they will be able to distinguish between *experiencing* the emotion of anger on the one hand and the way anger is dealt with or *expressed* on the other. With such an awareness they can begin to work on employing their anger constructively, instead of trying to eliminate it through suppression, denial, avoidance, or passivity. In addition, they can also avoid the opposite extreme of confusing assertiveness with aggression and believing that they should prevent being stomped on themselves by stomping on others first or in return.

To aid ministers in therapy to express anger assertively, mental health professionals need to help them examine the situations where anger occurs, possibly through taking a good inventory of themselves with respect to this emotion (see Table 2.1). By looking at the motivations, thoughts, feelings, and fears involved in different encounters, the therapist or counselor improves understanding and sets the groundwork for assertiveness.

Ministerial assertiveness is grounded on a belief that effective Christians can and should understand what makes them angry. They can and should be able to translate anger into a specific issue, and find the courage to recognize and remove unfinished business in their personality so the conflict area can be put into realistic perspective. They can and should be able

TABLE 2.1
Anger Recognition

Questions to help ministers achieve a better recognition of anger and indirect expressions of it (including passive aggressiveness), as well as motivations they might have with respect to uncovering and dealing with anger:

What did I get angry at today? (*Not*, what made me angry?)

With whom did I get angry today? (*Not*, who made me angry?)

In addition to the apparent reasons for my being angry or annoyed, what might be other reasons in me that would be responsible for the anger being so great?

How did I deal with my anger or annoyance? Did I try to conceal it? Did I deny it or play it down? Did I feel like covering it in a pseudo-Christian cover ("Don't get me wrong, I don't dislike him, just what he is doing to himself and the institution"; "I really feel he is misguided; he's really not a bad person")?

How did I spontaneously allow my anger to rise and come to the surface today without worrying it would cause other people to dislike me?

Was I able to review my anger and try to constructively deal with disagreements, with the understanding that communications won't solve everything, but that opening up a discussion about our differences is certainly a start? Or did I just try to scare people with my anger?

Did I present my anger to the source of it, or did I put the anger on someone else or make believe I wasn't angry?

to communicate their concerns to others in a manner which doesn't unduly raise defensiveness.

Ministerial assertiveness is also based on an appreciation that sometimes people are angry with others because their needs or expectations are unrealistic. When they are realistic, ministerial assertiveness calls for an openness, but one which doesn't justify being aggressive so they drive others away, and which doesn't glorify or prevent a free, real interchange. Instead, such openness allows angers to be dealt with as they arise, not when they blow up after a long period of being buried in a sea of "niceness." In essence then, therapists should feel free to vigorously intervene to uncover and help ministers in therapy deal with passive aggressiveness and indirect forms of anger, whether they are the recipients or are manifesting this maladaptive style themselves.

LONELINESS IN MINISTRY

That someone involved in intense ministry to others today might be lonely, seems impossible. Yet, given what we know about transference toward persons in helping positions, and the pressures present today for clergy and religious to perform well, the sad reality of the lonely minister is not so unusual.

Loneliness in ministry can involve the usual factors we encounter in helping people to move from loneliness to aloneness or solitude. However, it is helpful to look at some of the manifestations of loneliness as they appear in those in ministry.

Loneliness represents one of the emotional dangers when one lives a life of discipline as a helper. However, unlike many other helpers this discipline is wide-ranging. In other words, it is not just in the minister's office, the confessional, pulpit, or classroom that the minister must be in control and is filling a role designated by the community he or she serves. The minister often feels he or she must observe the same boundaries when in the rectory, at the hospital, when interacting with the parish staff, and even with most of his or her colleagues.

"Letting one's hair down" doesn't seem possible. After all, ministers will say: "Where can I blurt out my fears and sexual temptations?" "With whom can I trust my less than admirable behavior?" "When is it all right for me to curse, share my doubts about my faith, and bitterly criticize the church to which I belong?" And, "With whom can I discuss over a cup of coffee my sexual orientation and the decisions I have made around my sexuality?" Even the married minister must restrict "pillow talk" with a spouse. Unlike a telephone company supervisor who can discuss the aggravations of a day at the office, the minister cannot share anxiety or confusion about specific parishioners because of the realities of confidentiality and living in a close-knit community.

There are many issues which must be addressed if a minister hopes to remain a vital leader in the church today. And, like stress, loneliness is one of them. Just as often as the therapist hears comments such as, "I feel so overwhelmed; there is so much work to do," he or she will also hear, "I feel so cut off and alone. I have no one to share my little thoughts and feelings with each day."

Unlike members of a religious order or society which generally has people in ministry live together for support, the secular or diocesan Roman Catholic priests who are responsible for ministering in most parishes in the United States, are often alone. Because of the priest shortage in the United States the idea of the one-priest parish or even the one-priest per two parishes has come of age.

In such instances, priests such as these must be encouraged to maintain contact, even if it is via the phone, with other priests. In addition, close relationships of a nongenital type are now strongly encouraged with members of the opposite sex for heterosexual priests and with members of their own gender if they are homosexual. As will be addressed later in the chapter on celibacy, this is not always easy. But it is necessary if the person is to have a support network of friends who can supply the closeness that human beings need to survive and thrive.

Another problem in ministry in developing and keeping ongoing friendships as a way of avoiding unnecessary loneliness is that persons in ministry often get transferred. Such transfers can be to another part of the world in the case of some ministers, and across the country or the diocese for others. However, no matter how far, such disruptions are as difficult for ministers as they are for others who must constantly face such moves (i.e., military personnel).

Consequently, especially in the case of introverts, the situations can be difficult. The model we often see is of a person growing up, as an adult settling down and making friends, and continuing in his or her profession with a strong sense of support. This model is not a realistic one for ministers. Accordingly, they often need to be assisted in therapy in becoming more adept at separations and in making new connections when transferred.

Loneliness also results because of the failure to be able to let go of a role. The religious setting is an artificial world to some extent in which the minister is called upon to fill a role and do things that others are deemed not able to do as well. Expectations are high and the work quite demanding. Pulling out of that world and taking a human spot beside a spouse, other nuns if the minister is a nun, or at the table with other priests, is often quite difficult, especially since the others may be caught in a role themselves.

Friendships are also hard to maintain when one's schedule is so tight that others who also have their own demands to meet (especially other ministers) may not be able to arrange times to meet without a lot of preparation, and that then may fall by the wayside as well. In the case of married ministers, the minister's spouse may well be under a great deal of pressure because he or she has job-related duties along with the additional ones which come from being the pastor's partner in life.

Loneliness also arises out of constantly being surrounded by many people who are wishing to "borrow"—self-esteem, perspective, hope, and faith. The fog of depression, hostility, insecurity, and anxiety infects one with a sense of dread, doom, and loneliness if extra steps are not taken to get the support that is needed.

Since ministry is obviously not a well-paid profession, lack of financial resources also plays a part in loneliness. It is not as easy to travel, take leisure time with others, and take advantage of some pursuits which might mitigate the feelings of loneliness. A Protestant minister notes he would like to go skiing with his wife but his schedule is so full and he doesn't have the money to take the day trip to the mountains. A Catholic nun says she would like to visit a friend for the weekend but the house car is not free and she only gets $30 a month allowance so she doesn't have the money to rent a car for the trip. Money can well be an issue in loneliness.

Another factor is *time*. Ministers will often report real problems in getting the time to find, develop, and maintain friendships. One of the dangers in this is that the person may attempt to force a friendship with someone who has come in for spiritual guidance and thus lose any sense of boundary. Another danger is that the person may withdraw further. This "loner" stance can cause a loss of perspective and lead to an ongoing process of separation which can end in a dramatic step such as leaving the ministry on a whim with someone who seems to care for them. The married minister in a problem marriage is at risk to develop countertransference feelings for an attractive, empathic parishioner, and impulsively begin an affair that effectively ends the marriage and perhaps ministry itself. In other words, the minister embarks on a totally new life without giving the whole decision appropriate thought and consideration. Also, an ongoing process of separation leads for many either to depression or overinvolvement with self that produces narcissism and hypochondriasis (this latter condition being common among celibates).

On the other hand, if the person reacts to being alone with a sense of urgency or panic, then the danger lies in a belief that only a relationship will do. The danger in this case is that the person will fail to develop personal resources and self-esteem (including enjoying being alone), but instead will leap into any relationship or lose him- or herself in some group.

And so, in every psychotherapy experience with a person in ministry, sensitivity to loneliness and the interpersonal net that is present, is something worth exploring. Also, it is through the therapeutic relationship that the loneliness the minister is experiencing may be finally explored and faced so a new way of dealing with others becomes possible and productive.

A good example of this is the sexually abused minister. For instance, in the case of a female minister who was abused as a

child by her father, the style of behaving before insight into
the presence of abuse was one of "the good, dutiful little self-
sufficient girl."

However, after experiencing flashbacks she became depressed and fearful. This brought her to therapy where she
started to explore the abuse and deal with each of the stages of
uncovering the source and directions of it in the formation of
her style of dealing with the world. This eventually led to anxiety
and anger about the abuse.

In the course of treatment the therapist helped her structure ways to share the story of her abuse with two good friends.
With these friends she was able to be demanding, whiny, angry,
explosive, extremely dependent, and at times manipulative.
When she was in a position to accept the abuse as having been
part of her life and allow it to take a different place in her daily
focus, she also had energy to develop more and more assertive
approaches to relationships with others. In addition, interde-
pendency became possible in a new way as her self-esteem rose
and she could appreciate that as a child she was in no way
responsible for what happened and in turn these happenings
have no bearing at all on the wonderful person she was and
continues to be.

In this case, therapy was an excellent bridge to a new sense
of self so she no longer felt as needy as before. This is especially
important when one realizes that lonely people sometimes ema-
nate a sense of neediness which in turn pushes others away at
the very time when healthy relationships are needed. Breaking
negative cycles such as these are the grist of all therapy. However, they are particularly important possibilities in therapy
with ministers since their position in the community colors so
many of the other interpersonal relationships.

MARRIAGE AND FAMILY ISSUES

In this section, once again, our purpose is to highlight the
cultural issues related to working with ministers around marriage and family issues. We assume each therapist has his or
her own model for therapeutic interventions, so that we will
provide examples that illustrate the context that shapes marriage and family issues.

Life in a Fishbowl

At least three social influences exert considerable pressure on clergy families that create for them a sense of being under intense scrutiny. First, within each congregation several sets of norms, whether written or unwritten, encompass the expectations members of congregations have regarding the minister's family life. Each denomination has written or unwritten traditions that they expect clergy families to follow. These involve explicit ones such as rules regarding assignments, salary, the degree of centralized government, etc. Many churches, however, have less explicit traditions which members presume clergy families will observe. For example, the expectation that the minister's spouse host and coordinate the annual fund-raising picnic. When a minister assumes a new position in a congregation he or she may be aware of the explicit norms through the interview process or through reading policies and procedures. Many expectations for the family do not get communicated, but are, nonetheless, assumed by the congregation. From the standpoint of "informed consent," many families make a leap of faith when they follow the minister into a church assignment.

Second, these norms, whether derived from church policy or based on social expectations, exert powerful influence on family members. The norm of "proper conduct" expected of the family members will vary enormously from congregation to congregation. For one congregation "getting in trouble" may mean that the minister's teenage daughter smoked marijuana; for another it may mean she wore lipstick. The family members, therefore, live in a continual state of sorting out what is expected; separating out the essential from the trivial. Quite naturally, if a family member chooses to establish autonomy, the expression of that autonomy will often reflect thumbing one's nose at some church social standard. This, in turn, amplifies the tension for the minister.

Third, congregations closely observe the behavior of ministers and their families. This reality unfolds naturally, whether from the physical circumstances of living and working under the gaze of church members or from people's natural curiosity. Motivation for this close observation differs, but is nonetheless real. Some desire role models to guide them in the perennial struggle of inculcating religious values into modern life. Others develop a natural affection for the minister's family through simple association over time. Further, any group pays close attention to the well-being of its leader, since the group's own ability to thrive is closely linked.

It is useful, therefore, to appreciate that the social reality of the fishbowl need not develop from any inherent sense of malice, but may flow out of these benign or neutral motivations. However, just as overprotective parents create a stifling presence for children, ministers' families will experience the fishbowl, malicious or not, as oppressive.

> Madeline, a college student and 19-year-old daughter of a minister in a conservative Presbyterian church, had been dating a young man for about 9 months. On several occasions she had brought him to church with her for services as well as social events. People in the congregation liked Paul very much. He seemed polite, intelligent, and had a good sense of humor. Every Sunday that Madeline attended services members inquired about her relationship with Paul. When she and Paul decided to end their relationship, Madeline was unprepared for the visible looks of disappointment from church members. For months afterward people would ask her about Paul, with that slight hint in their voices that she perhaps had made a mistake. Thereafter Madeline made a point of never telling anyone whether she was dating anyone and certainly did not bring him around to church. In telling her story she was reflective on people's motives, and saw readily that no malice was intended. Rather, she concluded, for the congregation her life was more like an ongoing soap opera that provided a measure of harmless entertainment to them. She said it reminded her of when television fans would meet actresses on the street and question them about their screen romances as if they were real. In this case, however, Madeline's romances were real.

The "preacher's kid" reality intersects with children's and adolescents' normal developmental tasks. Their peers often belong to families of the minister's congregation. This makes it difficult to disclose the usual ups-and-downs of family life that children are wont to share. If they do disclose such matters, the minister's family will feel even more exposed.

Marital Issues

Although many of the marital issues discussed here apply to men and women spouses, because of gender role expectations the wives of ministers will often experience a more intense burden from social expectations than husbands do. For example, wives are commonly expected to teach Sunday school, sing in the choir, and provide leadership for the Women's Society or its equivalent. Wives are expected to provide food for bake sales and covered-dish affairs. For men and women much of the minister's social life revolves around parish activities, and the absence of a spouse is more noted than that of a member. Congregation members do not adjust these expectations when the spouse is employed outside the church or lacks interest in the church's social life.

The fishbowl existence has a profound effect on the spouse's (and family's) sense of comfort in their own home when they live in the parsonage, i.e., housing provided by the congregation. Spouses have an abundance of stories that detail the level of intrusiveness that is not tolerated in any other domestic situation in our culture. In many cases the congregation has a parsonage committee that is responsible for the physical care of the dwelling. When repairs are needed the family must obtain the committee's approval first, then they must wait for funds to be allocated, and, finally, hope for volunteers to arrive in a timely fashion to complete the work. Spouses note that they, furthermore, have to be "grateful" no matter how the work is done because the services are donated.

Should a spouse desire to change the decor, e.g., paint a room, the committee needs to visit and approve the request, *even if the family is paying for the material.* Homeowners who live under a neighborhood homeowners' association understand how making external changes to a house feels burdensome when awaiting the association's approval. One can only imagine the experience of intrusiveness when needing approval for *interior* changes as well.

Intrusiveness into family life is, at times, even more blatant. A wife described how once she was working in the kitchen when she was startled by an 8-year-old girl who ran in the back door. When questioned the little girl said she had to go to the bathroom. To her there was no need to knock, because the parsonage was hers. Another spouse described how, thinking she was alone in her home, she went downstairs in a bath towel after taking a shower to find three male parishioners repairing the furnace. Such experiences occur when multiple sets of keys to the parsonage are available.

In examining issues that typically evolve in clergy marriages we should not lose sight of the fact that the fundamental explanations for distressed marriages will be the same as in laypeople's marriages. Content and context may differ, but the process variables are similar. Researchers have concluded that the generic deficits in most distressed marriages include communications problems and an inability to solve problems (Beach, Sandeen, & O'Leary, 1990).

Stacy, age 32, married Bill, a Methodist minister,when both were in college. Although she was committed and satisfied with her desire to be an elementary school teacher, she also felt her life would be enriched by participation in her husband's ministry. She viewed this as a meaningful contribution that was also personally satisfying. She actively engaged in various church social and ministry activities and was well-regarded both for her role and the friendship she extended to many within the congregation.

When the couple's twins reached age 2, however, life began to look different. With two active boys in "the terrible twos," part-time work as a substitute teacher, limited funds for recreation and baby-sitting, she began to feel an increased need for emotional (and physical) support from Bill.

Bill found Stacy's complaints difficult to understand. Up until now he always viewed their relationship as a team effort. Often she was present at many of the functions he was required to attend, and he saw her as his confidant. Their "together time" involved getting ready for such events, attending them, and debriefing afterward. Their lives were intertwined, and he could not understand what more she desired. He knew she was often tired, but he was always willing to have her present in whatever group function was scheduled.

In this example the counselor's first task is to have the partners adequately communicate their needs to each other. Stacy's task is to be clear that the playing field for her has shifted substantially. She needs to describe what her energy boundaries are and what type of support she requires from Bill. Bill, for his part, needs to absorb Stacy's new situation. However, he also needs to make clear that their shared lives played an important role regarding its *relational* meaning. Whatever solutions or compromises they would reach would also have to address his intimacy needs as well.

Peter was personally indifferent at first to Mallory's decision to enter the seminary. He considered himself a "modern" husband, and if she wanted to be ordained, then she should have that right. Peter did not share Mallory's passion for her faith, either. Although raised an Episcopalian like his wife, his family seldom practiced their religion publicly, and by college Peter had drifted away from the church as an active force in his life. When Mallory went through her candidacy examination when applying to go to seminary, he told the evaluating psychologist that he would be supportive, but Mallory should not expect his life to change in any significant way as she pursued her career.

In the beginning the relationship continued to work for them. Although seminary studies were time-consuming, the couple usually had weekends free. Peter, furthermore, had at least an intellectual curiosity over what Mallory was studying, and they could discuss historical issues, if not the finer points of systematic theology. Even during her first assignment as associate pastor in a large urban parish, Peter adapted with minimal strain. He continued in his engineering position, the same job that gave enough financial freedom to support Mallory's studies and now her low-paying ministry position. Social life was good, for Peter loved city life, especially professional sports and being part of the company's basketball and football teams.

The strain began when Mallory received her first call as pastor in a small rural church, 45 miles from their home. Peter refused to relocate to the small parsonage available. Mallory needed to commute anywhere from 60 to 75 minutes to her parish. Since she often had evening and weekend activities, and returning home between events was wasted in travel time, she used the parsonage as a home base during the 12- to 15-hour days she was there.

Mallory felt enormous pressure to succeed. Her diocese was a relatively conservative one, and only due to the force of a financially astute and progressive bishop had women's ordination reluctantly been accepted. Furthermore, she received her call mostly because the low salary was unattractive and no male candidates applied. Indeed, the grapevine made it clear that had Mallory not accepted the call, the parish would have been forced to shut down. Not only was the diocese conservative, she was in the most conservative outpost of the diocese. The beginning had been hard, but gradually people had warmed up. Even the crusty head of the finance committee became her supporter after her guidance with a sticky medical decision for his terminally ill mother. Mallory found herself loving her work in a way she had never dreamed she would. She could see the impact of her pastoral care, and she knew that hearts that were turned against women priests were changing slowly but surely. Other women clergy from the diocese visited her frequently to garnish support in their struggles, and to receive guidance on how to walk the necessary tightrope of parish and church politics women ministers had to face.

Peter, however, felt abandoned. He admired his wife's success at some level, but his orphan status, as he viewed it, was totally unacceptable. Nearly every interest they once shared, from antique shopping to playing on the recreation center's mixed volleyball league, had ended. Their sexual life was a source of frequent conflict. Mallory was tired many days, especially on weekends when Peter tended to be most interested, or else Peter was asleep many evenings by the time Mallory came home. Mallory felt guilty about this and would sometimes go through the motions of making love. This usually backfired since Peter could sense her heart was not in it and he would lose interest himself. To complicate matters further, Mallory found her position changing on when or whether to start their own family. Originally she and Peter had wanted two children, but now she felt she might have the emotional energy only for ministry. Peter always envisioned himself as a parent and saw life unfolding for him in that role. If Mallory wanted to work for the church, that was fine; but her job was now interfering with their personal life in unacceptable ways.

This complicated case will require considerable communication and empathy on the part of both parties. The emotional pain that each experiences will first have to be addressed. Otherwise, attempts to problem solve too early will backfire. Mallory and Peter's story in its essential form is one that is common in marriage counseling. Its unique context requires the therapist to attend to the specific attributes of Mallory's occupation and, in particular, the personal and social meaning that it has for her. She finds it not only personally satisfying, but sees herself involved in something greater than her own self-fulfillment. At the same time she is sensitive to the relational demands of her marriage.

With all marriage counseling, but for clergy marriages in particular, it is important not to "split the difference" too quickly, i.e., come to a quick compromise. The guiding process should be one that tries to have each partner achieve as much of his or her needs as is possible. In the case of Peter and Mallory a quick compromise could easily miss a core ingredient for the partner's personal growth. Eventually this will sabotage the relationship.

THERAPY WITH INTERPERSONAL DISORDERS

Saboteurs of Community

Problematic interpersonal styles are the bane of religious communities whether in their membership or leadership. The famous "80-20" rule in management nowhere has more relevance than dealing with personality disorders in an organization. This rule states that managers direct 80% of their time and energy to 20% of the staff. In this section we want to limit our discussion to the personality characteristics already emphasized, including passive-aggressive as well as narcissistic, dependent, and avoidant features.

Ministers with any of these strong features follow a common career trajectory. Generally intelligent and verbally committed to the community's mission they fail to thrive in one assignment after another. Their resumé resembles someone attempting to enter the *Guinness Book of Records* for number of positions held. Everywhere the story is the same. Reverend or Sister starts an assignment and for a few months all is well. Eventually work performance suffers; sometimes because the person cannot handle the job duties, sometimes because of interpersonal conflict. Supervisors intervene resulting in temporary improvement, then the unsatisfactory pattern returns.

Everyone grins and bears it until the end of the contract or until everyone can save face. Reassignment in a year or two is the norm and the worker becomes some other community's headache.

This ability to easily find work for the person initially enables both person and community to duck the problem. Eventually communities run out of available positions or patience and a superior confronts the issue. Another barrier to prompt intervention is the culture of "niceness" we have described. A warm, accepting, nurturing community has enormous benefits and creates cohesion with the right mix. This environment, however, reinforces the negative patterns in personality disorders. Persons inclined to believe that the universe already asks too much of them will not spontaneously carry their own burdens much less assist others. An environment that is unfailingly willing to give second, third, and fourth chances plays into this negativity. Unlike the business community, which sees the bottom line as its motivation for dealing with incompetent workers, the religious community has a nonmaterial perspective. Criteria of success or failure are more nebulous. Repentance, not terribly valued in industry, buys considerable time in a faith community.

Somewhere in the process psychotherapy is recommended. Therapists need to appreciate the culture of such referrals to avoid one of two problems. The first is colluding with the pathology of the client. These clients generally lack insight and externalize their difficulties. They defensively blame the work setting, their superiors, or their peers for their own failures. They seldom present for treatment voluntarily, unless there are concomitant Axis I symptoms motivating them to seek relief. The referring community is tearing its collective hair out trying to cope with the minister. If the therapist's stance is one of noncommunication with the referring community, failure is guaranteed. Unlike treating addictions or sexual disorders, with this population *there is no smoking gun.* Our normal clinical digging to uncover some "real" problem is fruitless. Certainly one can always discover maladaptive developmental patterns in these clients, but their link with the work failure is tenuous at best. Often "what you see is what you get": a dependent, unmotivated, self-absorbed, passive–aggressive person who cannot work for a common goal within a group. Dialogue and feedback with the referring community is essential to understand this pattern and deal with it realistically.

A second problem relates to establishing the treatment goals. Therapists of all persuasions agree that brief therapy does not result in the characterological changes required. This leaves the therapist with two choices. Either select a short-term goal that will improve if not resolve the interpersonal style, or opt for long-term treatment oriented toward personality change. In either case ethical considerations dictate that the therapist discuss these options both with the patient and the referring community. When therapists choose long-term treatment informed consent demands that they describe outcomes accurately without creating false expectations of improvement. In the past, referring communities have passively complied with therapists' judgments in these matters. Nowadays, however, communities have expertise and will expect an honest dialogue with the therapist. Many also have had bad experiences related to excessive mental health care costs for these persons with little practical return. Taking an aggressive stance is natural since many communities are self-insured, or at least have substantial copayments when insured.

Treatment Guidelines

We suggest the following guidelines in working with personality disorders with this population.

1. For the reasons outlined above consultation with the referring community initially and at periodic intervals is essential for appropriate assessment. Communities often have personnel records that they are willing to share, such as number of assignments and performance evaluations. These tend to have much greater validity than client self-report. Since many ministers change geographical regions with new assignments, therapists should ask referring communities for information regarding the person's adjustment in those regions. Particular attention should be given to issues such as timeliness of performing duties, thoroughness, ability to carry one's work load,

and quality of interpersonal relationships. Problem areas tend to occur with anger management, attitudes toward authority, gender issues, and splitting of staff. In this way a comprehensive picture of the client emerges. It also prevents wasting time by relying exclusively on the client's self-report as the only data source.

2. Psychological testing has limits and benefits. Standard tests such as the MMPI often miss personality disorders, particularly when the person has little negative affect. Even those geared toward assessing personality disorders (e.g., Millon Multiaxial Clinical Inventory; Choca, Shanley, & Van Denburg, 1992; Millon, 1983) are spotty in our experience. We have noticed many false positives *and* false negatives confirming the need for multiple sources of information. We have found Five-Factor models of assessment useful (e.g., NEO-PI-R; Costa & McCrae, 1992; Piedmont, 1998). These measures describe important motivational dimensions for interpersonal functioning such as dutifulness, altruism, empathy, impulsiveness, angry hostility, rigidity in thinking, as well as the more traditional features of negative affectivity. The NEO provides added information because a coworker or friend can complete the test as an observer rating. Therapists can use this additional data to initiate dialogue around any discrepancy between self-report and the observer's perception of the client. Five-factor assessment tools translate easily into work and interpersonal behavior, data that also facilitate dialogue with referral sources. This is an advantage over connecting the more ambiguous output from traditional projective tests with performance predictions.

3. If the therapist takes on long-term treatment for personality disorders, treatment should focus on change-to-criteria. By this we mean that after a careful assessment of the client's work or interpersonal deficits, treatment goals should aim at specific behavioral objectives. We do not want to enter into the debate concerning the ultimate explanation of such personal deficits nor where in the person's metapsychology these forces lie. We are suggesting that change-to-criteria keeps the objectives clear for both client and referring community and provide easy-to-measure outcome criteria. Otherwise communities will

hesitate to support treatment goals that do not improve the person's adjustment.

In cases of deteriorating work performance we suggest the following. Set a criterion of competent job performance *outside* of ministry. If the client has had unfavorable performance ratings in the last few positions, insist that the client demonstrate the ability to perform satisfactorily in *any* work situation, except ministry. Attach a minimum time limit for demonstrating satisfactory performance before the client is eligible for ministry assignment. It may be appropriate for clients to work in a fast-food restaurant for one year just to demonstrate that they can get along with others, carry out orders, etc. Many times this is the only option left to leaders of sisters and brothers, since they cannot remove someone from the congregation simply for being inept in ministry. They can, however, use their authority to refuse to assign someone to pastoral work (i.e., work that has public religious meaning or endorsement), a sanction which has real bite even for those with personality disorders.

4. In our opinion the treatment modality of choice with such persons is group therapy. The traditional outpatient group that focuses on interpersonal experience in the here-and-now seems well suited for attaining interpersonal behavioral change. Groups should not consist only of religious professionals because they are prone to collude on issues of entitlement and the unfairness of authority. We prefer mixing religious professionals into groups with diverse membership. Often clients will strongly resist such groups, questioning how they can expect to be understood. In reality this is a disguise for the narcissistic features that contribute to their predicament. Mixed groups assist clients in self-confrontation, making it more likely that they will see the effects that their problematic behavior has on others.

Indeed the paradigm that Yalom (1995) follows in his classic text on group psychotherapy is precisely what these ministers require no matter what the treatment modality. First, they must come to understand what their actual interpersonal behavior is and how it comes across to others. Second, they must come to understand the broader meaning of this behavior. Do they act this way to keep people from getting close, to get others first before they are wounded, to make themselves comfortable, or because they see themselves as special? Third, they must decide if they are satisfied with this way of being. If they are not, then the change strategies can have some effect, whether through group or individual therapy. Individual therapy is handicapped in leading clients through these first two steps because it is so difficult to get the requisite behavioral sample from the client. That is why individual therapists must acquire large amounts of data from collateral sources when working with personality disorders in this population.

PART II

The Treatment of Negative Emotions in Religious Professionals
Anxiety, Depression, and Guilt

Negative emotions represent the primary reason for people entering psychotherapy. A major predicament for the therapist is to assess whether negative emotions result from aversive but flexible environments or represent an inability to adapt to truly inflexible ones. In this section we explore anxiety, guilt, and depression in the context of environments typical in ministry. We focus on skills needed for both sides of the equation: changing environments and changing moods. Only with an understanding of the minister's external environment and internal beliefs and assumptions can therapists apply normally effective interventions.

3.

Anxiety Treatment

In chapter 1 we examined the social culture that amplifies the experience of stress-related anxiety in our population. This included conditions known by such terms as *secondary stress, compassion fatigue,* and *vicarious* or *shared trauma.* Many themes discussed there are pertinent to managing anxiety, namely, limit-setting, life-style balance, preventing workaholism, challenging perfectionism, and defending against continual exposure to suffering and pain. In this chapter we will discuss anxiety as a clinical phenomenon and examine pertinent treatment interventions for the culture shared by religious leaders.

We will logically divide anxiety disorders according to the standard clinical, empirical one of fear and anxiety. In this framework fear relates to apprehension over an immediate environmental threat, and anxiety toward a future, often vague harm. As is customary in diagnosis, fear disorders include panic disorders (with or without agoraphobia), social phobia, posttraumatic and acute stress disorders, specific phobias, and obsessive–compulsive disorder. Generalized anxiety disorder will encompass most of our comments regarding treatment. Chapter 5 discusses obsessive–compulsive disorder incorporated more generally into issues of guilt (chapter 1 discusses the stress disorders in detail).

This chapter, then, will focus predominantly on anxiety management strategies. Since our book relates to the culture of religious professionals, our interest is in the cultural influences on diagnostic and symptom presentation. In panic disorder, for example, culture accounts for a small portion of symptom presentation, but for a large portion in the symptoms of generalized anxiety.

Similarly, we exclude extensive discussion of the specific phobias (e.g., fears of flying, animals, insects, injury or injections). The specific treatments via exposure and/or desensitization are straightforward and vary minimally from other populations.

However, we caution even here against overanalyzing. The apocryphal saying of Freud, "Sometimes a cigar is only a cigar," is often a wise guideline.

Hector, a seminarian in his midtwenties, entered therapy and described classic blood-injury phobia symptoms. He could not look at wounds, felt queasy when people described medical procedures they had experienced, and fainted at the sight of blood or medical paraphernalia. He worried because soon he would begin his fieldwork, some of which involved visiting the sick at home and in hospitals. Careful assessment required determining whether unsuitability for or dislike of ministry caused the phobic symptoms. When none was found, in vivo desensitization-exposure eliminated the fear and avoidance behavior. Follow-up contact revealed that many years later he continued successfully working as a pastor, routinely visiting parishioners in hospitals and intensive care units.

GENERALIZED ANXIETY

Anxiety, as is well known, plays both a functional and dysfunctional role in emotional life. In its functional role it serves, in psychologist Harold Liddel's poetic phrase, as "the shadow of intelligence." That is, it allows us to plan and make decisions for the future that cause us to prosper and avert untoward events: the education of our children, retirement, the coming of the tax collector, repairing a leaky roof. Neurology patients with prefrontal lobe disorders display little to no anxiety, yet can neither plan nor execute purposeful activity. Their social behavior is often crude and insensitive to others, although their basic intelligence is left intact. Here we are mainly interested in clergy plagued by an excess of anxiety, the type that impedes performance, is highly correlated with depression, and creates an internal experience of constant rumination, worry, and disquiet.

Anxiety: A Conceptual Framework

We can construe anxiety as a final common pathway triggered by multiple determinants. For the sake of organization we can conceive of three sources of anxiety that sometimes act independently but often converge into a single stressor.

Proximate Cognitive Causes

Aaron Beck refers to these sources of anxiety as automatic thoughts. Specifically, they represent two major types: The first overestimates the probability of negative events occurring; the second overpredicts the catastrophic consequences of a negative event if it were to occur.

Distal Cognitive Causes

In Beck's terminology these represent schemas, enduring mental styles that predispose people to react to certain kinds of stressors with anxiety-producing thoughts. One such schema relates to, e.g., the setting of performance standards, whether for self or others, that results in infrequent self-affirmation. Consequently, the person strives continuously to achieve flawless accomplishments. A second relevant schema is an excessive need to please or be liked by others. This results in social evaluative anxiety in situations both related to personal performance and wanting to belong.

Ineffective Behavioral Strategies

These have the effect of "painting yourself into a corner," and generating anxiety provoking stressors. We could identify much human behavior that qualifies for this category, and some we will discuss elsewhere (e.g., addictive behavior). We will limit this discussion to three specific ones.

Lack of Interpersonal Assertiveness

When the person regularly fails to assert interpersonal needs, he or she has to cope with situations that cause resentment or are unmanageable. This increases the sense of life's unpredictability and uncontrollability and generates significant anger.

Ministry preparation varies enormously both within and between religious denominations. Clinical assessment requires careful probing of each minister's educational background. Mainline denominations (Methodist, Episcopalian, Judaism, etc.) require postbachelor's theological training for their ordained ministers, usually involving 3 to 4 years at the master's level. In contrast some groups require only a bachelor's degree from a Bible college. Individual ministers could have other advanced degrees either from life prior to entering ministry, or for work in a specialized field. Catholic sisters and brothers have educational backgrounds that range from high school diplomas to advanced professional training.

Poor Planning and Organizational Skills

Poor planning and organizational skills often exist because the minister has either little education or supervised work experience in the areas of management. Many denominations offer little in the way of courses in business or management skills. Roman Catholic seminaries, for example, traditionally have had no courses in basic financial record-keeping, personnel management, law, or group leadership—building blocks to successful management.

The same criticism could be made of many professions, including the authors' own (psychology). However, unlike the typical psychologist, a pastor could oversee a church, school, and staff with scores of employees and budgets in the millions. That lack of preparation triggers significant anxiety should surprise no one. A second deficit is poor time management. With the multiple demands many are unable to delegate responsibility or establish goal-setting strategies such as management by objectives. This, in turn, diminishes self-efficacy, further intensifying one's lack of control.

Poor Problem Solving

Anxiety-prone individuals often fail to resolve predicaments by not using systematic decision-making methods. Cognitive science tells us that we make most of our life decisions (e.g., which breakfast cereal to purchase) by using mental shortcuts. These shortcuts exclude much of the information available. Nevertheless, we seldom suffer dramatically from these shortcuts because the database we use is often "good enough." We take these shortcuts for granted and forget that momentous decisions require substantial data. The standard problem-solving methodology described below and taught in business and science will accomplish this task, if the person remembers to activate it.

A cognitive, empirical model (Barlow, 1988) links anxiety to the two expectations of unpredictability and uncontrollability. When stressors are unpredictable, yet the person feels obligated to control them, anxiety is the likely result. When stressors are perceived as unpredictable *and* uncontrollable, depression overlays the anxiety as well.

CULTURAL UNDERPINNINGS

In the culture of clergy and religious, multiple factors contribute to the belief or reality of unpredictability and uncontrollability. In the occupational realm some congregational groups exercise near total control over their ministers. In hierarchical groups (e.g., Roman Catholics and Methodists) the religious leader has ultimate authority in assigning an individual. Even in these groups various degrees of consultation occur, representing a continuum of situations from the right to decline an assignment to having virtually no choice. Probably the closest analogy occupationally is the military, which reassigns personnel on a regular cycle.

However, a major difference between the military and clergy relates to promotion. Military personnel cope with frequent transfers, which involve family and personal stress, because transfers are associated with movement along a career track. In religious service transfer and promotion are not related. Roman Catholic associate pastors in large urban dioceses may have no chance of becoming pastors until they reach an advanced age, when people in most other work sectors are preparing for retirement. Although they will not lack for experience when they finally achieve pastor status, biological and psychic energy are diminished.

With shortages of clergy and religious in celibate groups, the issue of achievement or promotion is less salient, but alienation and overwork are. In Roman Catholic dioceses, where shortages of priests exist, promotion to pastor status occurs sooner than ever. Yet now the pastor often lives alone in a rectory without the support of brother priests as was customary a generation ago.

In many Protestant denominations, in contrast, the abundance of clergy and clergy applicants creates an opposite pressure. Here the critical issue is "receiving a call," competing against several candidates for a position in the congregation. Ministers are finding it more difficult to find attractive congregations, or, if in a church, discovering options for transfer to more suitable or challenging congregations.

Not every pastor, however, is beleaguered or suffering from burnout. In a study of American Baptist clergy, our colleague and former graduate student, Tom Rodgerson (1994), found low rates of burnout. These were senior pastors, the majority male, who reported considerable job satisfaction. He interpreted his findings as influenced by the considerable autonomy and independence enjoyed by veteran Baptist pastors. A cognitive, empirical model would predict that autonomy and independence would buffer the individual from stress-related disorders.

Contributing also to a sense of unpredictability and uncontrollability is the often ambiguous nature of the religious minister's role. Only recently have religious institutions adopted personnel policies and structures from secular work settings. In the past, often no job descriptions existed or, if they did, superiors did not follow them. Lines of authority often criss-crossed and a supervisor for one activity might be a colleague in another. Personnel records and official documentation are still Byzantine in many institutions. The net effect is to create a working climate that is often vague, involving multiple demands and inconsistent expectations, with no clear means of redress. Furthermore, personnel remain suspicious about the information available about themselves and procedures for its disclosure. Admittedly, this is a worse-case scenario, and various groups have arisen to address such concerns (e.g., National Association of Church Clergy Personnel).

For clinicians unfamiliar with the organizational structure of their clients a useful assessment strategy is to request from clients, in session or as a homework assignment, an organizational chart. Often clients need guidance in terms of delineating the structure, a process which itself is often diagnostic of the stressors. Organizational charts often resemble something drawn by the proverbial drunken sailor. One glance at the chart and all parties understand why the client feels out of control.

TREATMENT OF ANXIETY DISORDERS

Although we recognize the scientific limits of psychotherapy for establishing behavioral change, we maintain that the conscientious clinician needs to attend to the results of controlled clinical research for behavioral disorders. In clinical psychology this awareness has led to recent consensus statements regarding empirically validated therapies (EVT), for the purpose of providing clinicians with summary opinions about therapeutic approaches. In the spirit of this awareness we will incorporate

EVTs, when applicable, in our suggestions for treatment interventions with religious professionals. Treatment of generalized anxiety, in particular, follows an EVT, one developed by Michelle Craske and associates (Craske, Barlow, & O'Leary, 1992). One of us has adapted and modified this approach to incorporate spiritual or religious belief as an enhancement to the fundamental strategy (Ciarrocchi, 1995b).

This cognitive–behavioral framework understands excessive worry as linked either to overestimating the probability of some negative outcome, or to predicting that one could not cope with a negative outcome should it occur. Although the model maintains that *beliefs* essentially underlie worry, beliefs are not the only targets of intervention. In keeping with other research, changing *behavior* is often the most powerful route to changing beliefs. Therefore, we will describe a range of interventions, some cognitive, some behavioral, for anxiety reduction.

IMMEDIATE COGNITIVE SOURCES OF ANXIETY

The first step involves assessing the patient's belief system that generates anxiety. Assessment methods abound and readers can find sources in the references. The worksheet shown in Table 3.1 provides one example for having clients keep records of beliefs associated with their worries. The therapist can rapidly assess how the client overestimates the probability of a negative event or overpredicts an inability to cope with negative consequences. Once the client identifies the type of belief correlated with worry, the therapist guides the client through a process of restructuring or challenging these automatic beliefs. This, of course, represents standard cognitive–behavioral treatment.

For persons in ministry, however, many adjuncts exist that could powerfully enhance this restructuring or reattribution process. This strategy is a good match due to the higher than average level of intellectual skills in this group. Second, most spiritual perspectives evolve from a long process of wrestling philosophically with the great existential challenges: the meaning of life, death, loss, materialistic versus "higher" values, etc.

TABLE 3.1
Worksheet: Changing Worry With Spiritual Coping

Worry _____

_____

_____

Intensity Level _____

        0-1   = No worry
        2-3   = Mild worry
        4-5   = Moderate worry
        6-7   = Severe worry
        8-10 = Intense worry

Your Automatic Belief in Negative Outcome _____ (0 - 100%)

Negative Thinking About the Worry _____

_____

_____

_____

_____

_____

_____

_____

Spiritual Resources/Perspective	Personal Resources/Perspective
1. _____	1. _____
2. _____	2. _____
3. _____	3. _____
4. _____	4. _____
5. _____	5. _____

New Coping Thoughts/Perspective _____

_____

_____

_____

_____

_____

Realistic Probability of Negative Outcome _____ (0–100%)

Source: From *Why Are You Worrying* by J. W. Ciarrocchi (p. 48). Copyright © 1995 by J. W. Ciarrocchi. Reprinted by permission of Paulist Press.

Anyone versed in the intellectual content of the great religions comes with a worldview that creates meaning out of a seemingly capricious universe. Is it not curious that therapists so often ignore cognitive perspectives *that are readily available to their clients?* These perspectives could challenge the negative schemas from a stance that is at once authentic to and integral with the person's values. That mistake need not happen with this population. The therapeutic task is to elicit from the client these overarching worldviews that circumvent the anxiety-creating negative views.

What seems formidable here is the task of eliciting this worldview when, as therapist, you do not share or even know the client's spiritual perspective. This can be overcome in the same way any cross-cultural difference is managed. First, the counselor uses strategies to enter the client's inner world of meaning. Open-ended, nonjudgmental questions accomplish this by communicating a serious interest in the client's spiritual viewpoint. Acknowledging ignorance of the client's position can be a positive step toward developing a therapeutic alliance. From this admission the counselor takes a "please teach me" approach toward the client's framework. Meichenbaum (Meichenbaum & Cameron, 1983) describes this as a "Columbo-like" questioning strategy, named after the television detective who gathers much information by playing dumb. The difference here is that the therapist is truly unaware. Listening intently to the client's automatic thoughts allows the therapist to help the client connect cognitive assumptions with the situation triggering anxiety.

The worksheet shown in Table 3.1 provides one method for eliciting overarching worldviews. Instead of imposing adaptive beliefs on the client, this record sheet allows client and therapist to work on perspectives that challenge the tendency to overestimate and overpredict catastrophes.

Pastor Jane is an effective, well-liked associate pastor in a thriving Methodist church. From her own perspective, however, life requires constant vigilance to prevent the untoward events she believes are perpetually threatening to alight upon her domain. She is a continual worrywart, but has difficulty seeing the cost to herself of this ever-watchful stance: frequent stomach upsets, tension headaches, irritability with friends and associates. She seldom takes a vacation, even though her church council has urged one. Too often her day off involves taking care of a few pieces of business prior to getting out of the parish office. The regional bishop will visit next week, two days after her scheduled day trip to New York with her best friend to see a musical. As the time for the visit drew closer, Jane worried that all would not be ready, and if she left she could not prevent a potential mishap from marring the occasion.

The intervention model described here suggests the following strategy for dealing with Pastor Jane's immediate anxiety. Begin with a self-monitoring device such as the worksheet in Table 3.1. Ask Jane to contemplate what sorts of problems she anticipates. She then records what degree of probability she is estimating that these events will happen. Generally persons become anxious in such situations because they attach a high degree of probability to these events, when in reality the probability is much smaller. Discuss with her the actual rather than the anticipated probability of these negative events occurring. Have her record the estimated probability that follows from a thorough, realistic discussion of the situation. For example, what kinds of things could go wrong? How often have they gone wrong in the past? Given all that she is doing, could she prevent them from happening anyway? Who is also keeping an eye out for such a problem? How picky is the bishop anyway, etc.?

A second prong is for her to follow through on the "what-if" aspect of the situation. What if some negative event occurred during the bishop's visit? How, in reality, would she and other members of the congregation handle it? What would the bishop's likely response be? What would its actual impact be on her, the congregation, the church, the furthering of God's will? In this manner she is dealing with the second automatic thought that relates to generating excessive anxiety through catastrophizing. Catastrophizing implies that if something negative were to happen, I could never handle it. Exploring this belief systematically will allow Jane to reflect on unattended strengths, both within her environment and within herself, that enable her to cope with untoward events.

An auxiliary approach is to ask Jane to reflect upon ways in which her theological worldview might combat her propensity to ignore self-care. As clinician you are clear that her failure to live a balanced life-style creates vulnerability to stress. What reminders from her faith experience could help her view self-care as essential, not something for stolen moments and resulting in a guilty conscience? Consider this approach in the following case:

> Sara, a Lutheran pastor of a small inner-city congregation, is overwhelmed by what feels like 24-hour-a-day demands as a church leader and mother of two preschool boys. Although Sara was fully versed in her biblical tradition, her therapist suggested a homework assignment with a slight twist. Sara should read one chapter daily of the Gospel of Mark. But she was to pay attention to how often Jesus (1) rested or took time off; (2) went off to pray; or (3) allowed someone else to do something pleasant or caring for him. She returned to therapy with the insight, "He hardly did anything." Further, with a feminist deconstruction of the first-century religious community, she noted how often it was that women did things for him.

Jane, therefore, might similarly begin to focus on the scriptures. She might be asked to examine those that deal directly with worry; e.g., "Consider the lilies of the field, they grow; they toil not, neither do they spin." This will allow her to integrate the cognitive–behavioral strategies discussed above with holistic reflections buttressed by her personal spiritual resources.

PERVASIVE COGNITIVE ANTECEDENTS: GENERAL COMMENTS

From a cultural context the above clinical example illustrates a major interpersonal style that has within it the seeds for a variety of emotional ills. An excessive need to please is the bane of many in ministry. It arises both as a personality style and a committed belief. Research suggests that people in ministry have large amounts of what the Five-Factor model of personality terms *agreeableness*. This quality represents a concern for pleasing others, avoiding conflict, going along with others' wishes, or mediating differences between people. It enables the minister to show concern for others, express empathy, and get along with a variety of complex personalities. For many this quality is prescribed as an important spiritual value. The Christian theologian Dietrich Bonhoeffer described Jesus as "The Man for Others," a description that remains a model for religious leaders. Love of neighbor, which is the hallmark of nearly every religious group, further prescribes this stance of openness and acceptance of others.

A second dimension, strongly reinforced culturally, that provides a fertile soil for the seeds of anxiety is perfectionism. Many divergent strains coalesce to create strong expectations upon those in ministry to conform to the highest imaginable standards of personal and professional rectitude. A friend of our teenage daughter was visiting as one of us was writing this book, and asked its purpose. Upon hearing the topic she said, "I hope I'm not speaking out of line, but aren't clergy supposed to be, like, messengers of God. Aren't they close to God in a special way, and don't they, like, hear him speaking to them more than the rest of us?" In her direct way this young woman captured a host of conscious and unconscious cultural expectations of religious professionals. In the Christian tradition the religious individual hears it quite directly in the Gospel injunction, "Be perfect as your heavenly Father is perfect."

Both these qualities, excessive need to please others and perfectionism, have been identified as being at the root of multiple emotional problems. In particular, both anxiety and depression are seen as related to these concerns (Blatt, 1995). We will focus mostly on the social, evaluative dimensions of these qualities and consider perfectionism as a personality characteristic under the section on depression.

An excessive need to please others can be understood from a variety of psychological models. We will mention two for their clinical utility. Aaron Beck (Beck, Freeman, & Associates, 1990) has described the quality of *sociotropy* as being implicated in psychopathology. In his framework, sociotropy describes a schema, i.e., a stable, fixed belief, which surrounds the desire to please others. When people have this to an extreme degree their lives are characterized by anxiety and depression, to name but two negative consequences. For Beck, a schema, unlike an automatic thought, operates much like a personality characteristic. If the boss has her head down when I pass her in the corridor, I may begin to wonder if I displeased her. Either an automatic thought or schema may have generated this perception. If I generally tend not to worry about my relationship with her, but today read a newspaper article on corporate downsizing, my upset is a situation-limited automatic thought. However, if I tend to be hypervigilant for signs of the boss's displeasure, then a pervasive schema is operating. Clinicians need to assess whether anxiety from interpersonal upset is episodic and situational, or chronic and pervasive.

A second model for understanding an excessive need to please others comes from the work of developmental psychology, particularly the work of John Bowlby and Mary Ainsworth (Ainsworth & Bowlby, 1990; Bowlby, 1988). Their model, attachment theory, examines the developmental antecedents of such characteristics as needing to please others. Attachment anxiety stems from unstable primary caregivers in early childhood. Children with stable, available caregivers explore their environments with minimal anxiety since they have a "secure base." This base gives them the necessary self-confidence to investigate novel events. When caregivers are either unavailable or inconsistent, problematic interpersonal styles develop. Sometimes, when real or perceived abandonment from caregivers occurs, compulsive self-reliance develops, an interpersonal style that seeks minimal engagement with others. In the second instance, when caregivers are inconsistent an anxious, dependent style emerges.

> Father John, a young Episcopalian priest, labors anxiously over each sermon. He regrets not only the amount of time he puts into sermon preparation compared to his peers, but also the mental battle with his nerves during the entire process. He finds himself obsessing over each sentence, wondering how acceptable it will be to the members. He actually focuses on the congregation according to their theological positions of conservative, liberal, or middle-of-the-road. He imagines how each camp will read every point he makes. This procedure came about from

the feedback he received after his first few sermons. One week some conservative members said he was neglecting doctrine; another week liberal members complained that the Bible does not have every answer for this century. He observed with some horror a creeping writer's block that was close to causing paralysis.

Clinicians familiar with treating social phobia will understand the dynamics of this writer's block. However, Father John may have resources available for challenging these assumptions that the therapist may not appreciate. For example, questioning him about his own religious model might be fruitful. Did Jesus ever have difficulty with congregations? Did he ever preach messages that were not accepted by 100% of his listeners? How did he react when this occurred? (In fact, Jesus said his disciples should put rejection behind them; "shake off the dust under your feet," as a testimony against people who would not receive their message.) As the client begins to link preaching with some degree of rejection, the therapist inquires how awareness of this selective rejection might help when writing the next sermon. Using a record sheet such as the worksheet in Table 3.1 is one way Father John can focus his alternate belief concretely, and have it available when he writes sermons.

An anxious, dependent attachment style is at the heart of both dependent and avoidant personality styles. Dependent persons cling anxiously to others for fear of their own emotional survival. Avoidant persons also have deep dependency needs, but are so rejection-sensitive that they only enter into relationships with unusual guarantees of acceptance. This is illustrated in the *New Yorker* carton that has the chic young lady telling her male companion, "If you really loved me, you would dump me."

The culture of religious professionals often reinforces dependency issues. In some Protestant congregations the minister serves completely at the discretion of the congregation which hires and fires. Under these circumstances the disposition to please as large a constituency as possible is not an "irrational assumption" (Ellis & Harper, 1975). Congregations routinely terminate pastors who fail to serve the congregation's wishes. There are few analogous situations in the business world. Most organizations have boards that independently look to the needs of the corporation. Many pastors are in situations that are analogous to a university where the students have the authority to hire or fire the president. Imagine a president in this situation needing to make a decision to lengthen the school year. Religious professionals frequently develop hypervigilance to real or imagined criticism. This, in turn, leads to catastrophic reactions when even a single member disagrees or disapproves.

At the other extreme, the regional superior determines assignments, and individual congregations have little say over personnel decisions. In such circumstances overdependency may result in losing personal initiative, resourcefulness in problem solving, or expecting others to solve one's problems. Much of the time a tendency toward dependency in the clerical environment remains functional. I recall a woman observing two men in her apartment building who had recently left the seminary. She was amazed at how they obtained a variety of financial benefits and ample amounts of food from the elderly widowed landlady. As Millon has noted, one strategy for coping with life is to become plantlike: find a spot that has nurturing soil, food, water, and sunlight, then stay put. This mentality leads to anxiety, however, when nurturing is either threatened or absent and people have to fend for themselves minus essential skills.

TREATMENT OF PERVASIVE COGNITIVE ANTECEDENTS

Assessment

The first step in treating dysfunctional schemas is assessment. Both cognitive and attachment theories are useful here. Attachment theory suggests that the perceived overprotective or inconsistent parenting styles lead to interpersonal dysfunction. Clinically this pattern emerges either as a "not wanting to leave the nest" in terms of interpersonal risk taking, or an anxious-ambivalence regarding relationships. The first pattern expects others to take care of all of one's needs. Further, the expectation often is accompanied by the belief that others will somehow intuit one's needs without one giving voice to them. In the second pattern the person is rejection-sensitive and clings desperately to others. These patterns can be assessed via history taking of relationships, paying special attention to their number, quality, and how the client dealt with endings. Does the person rebound within a reasonable period or do they remain gun-shy? What expectations do they have about relationships? How much or how little should others be available?

Cognitive theory is useful in assessing the day-to-day impact of expectations that have resulted from these attachment patterns. Using the standard recording sheets from Beck or Burns (Beck, Rush, Shaw, & Emery, 1979; Burns, 1989) may simplify this process, or even using the worksheet from Table 3.1 above may serve the same purpose. We need to point out that no empirical data exist on the most effective means for tracking automatic thoughts or schemas, so clients have wide latitude in a recording method. In any cognitive assessment, schemas will be idiosyncratic. Simply because an expert identifies certain themes in the schemas of dysfunctional emotions, does not mean your client will have that exact theme. A minister, who mistakenly believed that her husband was interested in pornography, revealed that her upset related to her husband thinking about another woman during sex. This came out in marital therapy during reflective listening. The husband was astounded she could think this of him. This belief surprised the therapist as well who had believed her discomfort rested on moral grounds. Only patient assessment reveals personal schemas.

Restructuring Negative Schemas

Coping with dependency-related anxiety schemas requires restructuring these belief systems. This strategy is efficient because many diagnoses are related to overdependency schemas. The following represent a handful: interpersonal conflict, adjustment disorders, anxiety disorders, addictive behavior, mood disorders, and personality disorders. Working directly on the cognitive schemas may be a direct path for improving any of the above diagnoses.

The strategy developed by Beck (Beck et al., 1979) provides one avenue to changing schemas that is minimally burdensome. Briefly, clients self-monitor incidents around interpersonal situations that trigger emotional upset. For each event they record the following information: (1) description of the event; (2) self-statements or automatic thoughts at the time; (3) degree of upset (e.g., on a scale of 1–10); (4) the resulting negative emotional or behavioral consequences following the incident.

As they gather information regarding these events, through processing them in therapy and self-reflection, general themes start to emerge. Beck (Beck, Freeman, & Associates, 1990) has described typical assumptive schemas that relate to overdependency. Such schemas include a need to be affirmed and approved of by nearly everyone; the notion that it would be catastrophic if others do not like or think well of you, etc. Many of Beck's schemas resemble the "irrational ideas" Albert Ellis depicted earlier as the source of emotional upset.

We note a common technical error that clinicians make by applying Beck's or Ellis' method too mechanically. Sometimes clinicians use the schemas or irrational ideas deductively with clients once they have assessed a problem with overdependency. For example, once intense social-evaluative anxiety has been identified, some therapists hand out a list of cognitive distortions to help clients challenge their excessive need for approval. Clients, then, are to "challenge" or "restructure" these distortions to make them more "realistic" or "rational."

At least three problems flow from this approach. First, individualized self-monitoring will convince you that clients' assumptive schemas can be amazingly idiosyncratic. Some will have schemas that resemble those identified by Beck and Ellis, but often the belief system is highly personalized.

Brother Phil suffered burnout after 8 months of 60–80 hour work weeks overseeing the construction of a multimillion dollar sports complex at a large university run by his religious order. When he was forced to take off after a stress-induced anxiety attack he processed in therapy the source of his driven work habit. He was a Vietnam veteran who had actually reenlisted for duty having served in a dangerous war zone as a combat Marine.

He felt obligated to reenlist because he believed he had identified strategies for combat survival. His sense of carrying out the Marine mission of "never letting your buddies down" carried over to staying in the military to save lives by sharing his experience. He began to connect for himself his intense work habits with this sense of "not letting others down."

Here no list of canned distortions could ever lead back to his assumptive schema. Schemas have to be uncovered inductively, by "guided discovery," to use Beck's phrase, not prescribed to clients. They need to emerge as part of the assessment and data-gathering process before effective restructuring can occur.

A second problem with proceeding deductively is that it is more likely to generate resistance or countercontrol than if one proceeds inductively. Client acceptance of underlying assumptive schemas is more likely when schemas flow naturally from the self-monitoring process.

A third problem arises from viewing client schemas as "distortions" or "irrational." Social cognitive theory has shifted perspective on this issue, and indeed demonstrates that on certain tasks depressed people are *more* realistic than nondepressed people in their cognitive judgments; that is, they are more likely to judge accurately the control they have, particularly over positive outcomes. Therefore, an approach that labels client schemas as irrational may lead to defensiveness. The therapist can help clients see the *implications* of maintaining a particular perspective. In the above example Brother Phil saw that if he continued to view the situation in the same way, he would rapidly exhaust himself mentally and physically, and ultimately let down everyone. The therapist did not need to attack his belief that he should not let his buddies down. He needed to see that *the way he was interpreting that belief* caused immense self-harm and ultimately sabotaged the value it stood for.

After careful assessment of the assumptive schemas, therefore, restructuring is the path to counteract their effects. As for personality influences, persons in ministry often are high on agreeableness, meaning they often put others first. If they self-monitor a variety of incidents, they may see how this characteristic even takes on a religious flavor. In a workshop on dealing with troublesome personalities in congregations, the ministers arranged themselves into small groups to develop prototypical cases of difficult people they had encountered. The workshop leaders then used the cases to brainstorm problem-solving strategies. After listening to the participants describe their woes in dealing with difficult personalities, one clergyman shared his relief. He summarized the burden he had felt up until then. "I have been a pastor at several parishes, and, inevitably, I have always run into two or three of these people. I had always concluded that these people acted this way because I had failed as a pastor to create a truly Christian community." When asked by the workshop leader to elaborate on how he then ended up feeling, he replied, "I was demoralized because I saw myself failing as a pastor."

Therapists may have difficulty dealing with religious people who have such deeply embedded beliefs. The idea that one could *value* self-abnegation is often foreign. Furthermore, therapists will encounter endless (and needless) struggles if they try to change this belief directly. The best strategies are indirect ones that evolve out of the client's self-awareness. One approach is to allow clients to decide if the belief is possible to fulfill. For example, how is the need to please everyone or be available to everyone playing out in practice? Are they successful? Are they acting in a truly loving fashion? Generally the answer will be no. If they were truly satisfied, they would not likely be in therapy.

Sometimes, if the therapists are familiar with the client's religious perspective, they can use this information after the client restructures the belief. For example, the "great commandment" in both Jewish and Christian law is that you should love the Lord God with your whole heart, mind, and soul; and your neighbor as yourself. Some have noted that self-love is one-third of the equation here. Again, you will meet resistance if you try to prescribe self-love. Self-love is palatable to clients when they realize their need to take care of others caused endless anxiety and self-absorption. Self-absorption is the antithesis of love.

TREATING BEHAVIORAL DEFICITS

Poor Planning and Time Management

Planning and time management deficits result in a disorganized and chaotic life-style that amplifies worry and anxiety even for those in ministry without clinical anxiety disorders. The cultural bugaboo here is the pastoral idea of availability. Ministers frequently interpret the pastoral value of availability to mean being continually accessible to those in need. Several negative effects flow from this mentality and its related practices. Availability and accessibility become priorities so that scheduled events are either eliminated or put off. Important tasks, then, are not completed or not given their deserved attention. Management practice degenerates into an expectation that somehow the "Spirit" watches over everything. Long-range planning and goal-setting almost represent a failure to honor the Spirit.

Perhaps more serious is that ministers with these expectations are prone to lead a life without boundaries. Necessary personal pursuits are neglected: health issues (medical and dental appointments); recreational needs (exercise, planned vacations); social needs (maintaining nurturing relationships); and family obligations (deepening marital intimacy, being present to children). A life without boundaries too easily evolves into patterns of high-risk behavior. A strong correlation exists between such life-styles and proneness to compulsive, acting-out behavior. As we shall see in treating such behaviors, they function initially as effective stress-relief mechanisms that require little time or social involvement. A trip to a massage parlor or the racetrack, or a drink all provide quick tension-reduction. They demand minimal planning and initially can fit into hectic schedules.

Time management and planning are the obvious remedies for such a life-style. Any number of methods are effective and should be tailored to the inclinations of your clients. Some do perfectly well with simple systems such as Alan Lakein's *How to*

Get Control of Your Time and Life (1973), an inexpensive paper-back that almost all systems imitate. More elaborate systems are available in any office supply store. Whatever system clients choose the principles are similar.

Choose Goals

Lakein suggests breaking goals down into long-term (5-year) and short-term (1–2 years). For persons having difficulty setting priorities he suggests the following exercise. Imagine that you have just been told that you have a terminal illness. It will not affect your physical or mental capacities until the very end but you will die in exactly 6 months. What would you choose to accomplish in those 6 months? This exercise helps people focus on their values and priorities.

Develop Planning Skills

This requires long- and short-range skills. Long-range planning requires reviewing goals periodically (perhaps monthly) to see if they have changed, and adjusting them accordingly. Short-range means setting aside time weekly and daily to plan for immediate events. Weekly planning reviews the needs and goals for the coming week. Daily planning focuses on today in detail. The critical clinical tasks here are evoking a commitment from the client to follow through with you on the nitty-gritty of the scheduling process. A vague commitment to plan seldom works. The therapist needs to instruct, and when necessary, review the monthly and weekly schedules. In this way one will know how well the client is setting aside the necessary time to plan.

A natural resistance to planning comes from two sources with religion professionals. One is the perception of the burden of having to do "one more thing" in an already overburdened life. We do not advise attempting to persuade, or still worse, argue with a client over this issue. Clients can view this as an "experiment" to figure out its utility. Usually, however, the payoff is immediate. The more common problem is sticking with the system even when its benefits are quite apparent. A second form of resistance comes from the belief that living a life of service requires not being tied down to schedules but being open and available to the needs of others as they arise. Again, instead of persuading or arguing, ask the clients if their current schedule allows the availability they want. Are they or their parishioners content with how available they are? Is their time organized efficiently to allow them to spend enough time preparing their sermons, servicing the poor, attending to the ill, counseling the distressed, and managing administrative duties? If they are satisfied, they are not in need of time management. If they are not satisfied, however, then you could invite them to explore methods that allow greater efficiency.

One major barrier to effective time management in ministry, which is often not addressed in the commercial programs available, is the routine nature of interruptions in the minister's life. Therapists should help ministers distinguish between two types of interruptions, the avoidable and the unavoidable. The avoidable ones derive from unreasonable demands for the minister's presence; whether at meetings, celebrations, or to attend to a need that is a "crisis" only in the mind of the parishioner. Dealing with these issues is not so much one of scheduling and planning but one of assertiveness. Typical beliefs underlying the minister's hesitation in setting personal limits were addressed in chapter 1. The second type of interruptions, however, do require creative scheduling. Ministers cannot do long-range planning around funerals, parishioners' illnesses, or the genuine crises that are part of normal pastoral work. Time management specialists suggest that under such circumstances a rigid schedule is as ineffective as a loose one. In these situations planning around a 3-week time frame is recommended. The minister should list the number of events and tasks that are reasonable to accomplish within that time frame. The schedule should have a reasonable number of empty spaces to accommodate the juggling required in the minister's real world. With this process the minister will not feel unduly frustrated when schedules need adjusting, nor will priority tasks get ignored when emergencies arise.

Monitor and Adjust

Planning, by definition, involves continual monitoring and adjusting to life's changing demands. The therapist's monitoring of the client's planning and scheduling assures that the client develops this independent skill. Effective change, however, means never leaving generalization of skills to chance or hope.

Problem Solving

Seminary or other forms of ministry training often neglect courses in general business strategies. Unless the religious professional enters ministry with a background in business or management, he or she may not have exposure to formal problem-solving strategies. Ten years experience in teaching courses in group dynamics to pastoral counselors confirms the absence of problem solving as a formal skill. Effective problem solving improves one's self-efficacy which, in turn, bolsters one's sense of personal control. Many sources in both the business and psychological literature describe the steps in detail. Briefly they involve: (1) Identify the problem(s); (2) Generate solutions(s); (3) Evaluate solutions(s); (4) Select solution(s); (5) Carry out the solution(s); (6) Evaluate the outcome and adjust.

Appropriate uses for such a strategy in ministry settings might include: complicated personnel decisions; financial difficulties; marital conflict (once the couple displays basic skills in communication); and facilitating group process for a committee or organization.

The therapist should not assume that because persons in ministry are educated and accomplished, problem solving is readily available as a personal management skill. A marriage counselor was seeing Reverend Bradley, an Episcopalian priest, and his wife Elaine, who was executive vice-president of a moderate-sized corporation. The couple could not agree over the merits of private versus public school for their children so the counselor initiated problem solving. When the counselor moved into the detailed explanation the couple broke into laughter. They explained they had given many talks on this topic together in their premarital counseling sessions and marriage encounter retreats. This experience of "Physician, heal thyself" suggests that the therapist should not assume skills already in clients' repertoires are available for their use.

Assertiveness Training

A close relationship exists between anxiety and unassertiveness. Anxious persons feel taken advantage of, fail to stand up for themselves, and avoid both conflict and intimacy. Repeatedly we have pointed out that the culture of chronic niceness is one that hampers religious professionals in many areas.

Clergy and religious may respond unassertively for one of two reasons. In the first instance they may lack the requisite interpersonal skills to handle the situation. For example, they may want to obtain a position as a chaplain, but until now their religious superior has always assigned them to a position. For this job they will have to go through a competitive interview process and they feel awkward playing up their accomplishments. They see modesty as a virtue and would not think to list some relevant skills on their resumé, much less talk about them. Another example relates to dealing with conflict. Accustomed to mediating conflict, they fail to understand that dealing with certain behavior (e.g., passive-aggressive) requires direct confrontation, a style that feels mean or insensitive in the standard of clergy culture. Yet failing to deal assertively leads to manipulation and feeling angry, depressed, or anxious.

In the second instance the minister has the requisite skill but anxiety inhibits use in the specific situation. In this situation the minister may attend to his or her limits and refuse requests from others. The minister certainly has the interpersonal skill and prerequisite vocabulary to utter the effective phrase, "No." Here expectations of hurting the other's feelings or some other anticipated negative outcome inhibits its expression.

In both situations assertiveness training can be effective. Training can occur informally via role-playing during the session. The therapist may be familiar with the cultural context so questioning and scene-setting is important. An effective way to understand the context is for the counselor first to take the client's role and have the client play the other party. This allows the therapist time to figure out appropriate responses to model for the client. After playing this scene until it is accurate, client and therapist reverse roles so that the client can practice the relevant dialogue.

If the minister lacks a wider range of interpersonal skills, more formal training may be required, whether in specialized groups, adult education workshops, or formal group therapy. It may seem odd that a profession that emphasizes public speaking has members with significant public speaking anxiety. The therapist who works with seminarians or young ministers will frequently encounter public speaking anxiety, either alone or with other social phobia symptoms. Besides the cognitive–behavioral strategies outlined in this chapter, referral to Toastmasters International is also effective. This is a nonprofit support group that helps members build public speaking skills. This group has several advantages: low cost; it trains to criterion (i.e., public speaking); clients interact with others who share the same problems; the affirmation increases members' confidence in other social settings. Seminarians report they enjoy it because they feel they can be themselves, not a representative of a religious organization. Our experience suggests that identifying a social phobia and treating it when candidates are still in training or seminary prevents paralysis at a later point.

4.

Depression and Mood Disorders

At Sunday worship service a visiting priest is officiating, He delivers a stirring and warm sermon that so moves the congregation it erupts into applause, something that has never happened in this church. More astounding is the revelation at the end by the church deacon that Father learned right before the service that the community was celebrating concern-for-the-homeless Sunday. He had prepared a sermon on a different theme. Again the congregation applauds. This scene is remarkable, for unknown to any in the congregation, this minister spends several hours a week staring at a large kitchen knife contemplating suicide.

This case illustrates several features common to depression for clergy and religious professionals. The condition remains hidden with the sufferer going to enormous lengths not to let on, even with intimates, about the degree of pain. Although they can keep it together outwardly for select activities, sufferers will crash when not propped up situationally by some ministerial task. Finally, clergy and vowed religious are no more immune from suicidal ideation or impulses than any other group, no matter how proscribed by their religious belief system. Some circumstances *increase* the risk. In the United States several Roman Catholic priests have committed suicide following investigations of sexual misconduct with minors.

The preeminent clinical characteristic of depression with this group is the sense of shame in the sufferer. Shame, although common in depression with any group, often takes on a particular cultural twist. Religious professionals often view depression as a sign of God's judgment. On occasion this may take the form of seeing it as a punishment for some misdeed. Here it more closely resembles the psychodynamic notion of guilt as the result of some transgression.

More often, however, it exists as true shame, i.e., a failure of one's ego-ideal that one has not lived up to essential expectations. Here the sufferer views the very existence of the depression as failure. Underneath this is the expectation that a true person of God would never succumb to such feelings. This comes partially from a theological tradition that sees despair as the moral opposite of the virtue of hope. Consumed by the negative triad that views the world, the self, and the future as hopeless, the person cannot distinguish the intense feeling of hopelessness from the judgment of despair described in moral theology. Moral despair involves a lack of trust, a belief that God is unavailable; while the despair suffered in depression begins as a "dark night of the soul," a sense of absence. Poetry attempts to capture this distinction. In Francis Thompson's *The Hound of Heaven* (1958), God pursues the despairing person who is trying to make sense of the blackness. When finally the person experiences God he questions God's absence during the darkness. The poet hears that the darkness was God's shadow hovering over the person.

As with other fixed psychological notions, rational argument is often futile. Unsolicited affirmation regarding the person's ministerial effectiveness does not sink in. The strategy may backfire with the severely depressed. "See," is one common response, "I am a despicable hypocrite who can fool people into thinking God works through me."

Shame, then, can infect every aspect of treatment with religious professionals. They even may view taking antidepressants as an example of their moral weakness. "If I truly trusted in God," goes their logic, "I would not need this crutch." We are not describing here religious groups who oppose standard medical interventions on theological grounds, but persons otherwise accepting of medical care.

They may also resist the psychosocial strategies we suggest below because they believe they will scandalize the faithful if they share their own despair. Rational–cognitive therapies that challenge this shame head-on risk degenerating into endless theological debates. The therapist, simultaneously, is usually at a disadvantage here. The client may not trust the therapist's religious background to challenge such a delicate area. From a cultural context the therapist may not understand the precise conceptual background the client brings to his or her experience.

Interpersonal therapy provides an avenue for effective entry into helping the client change an environment that supports depression. As an empirically validated therapy, research finds it equally effective as antidepressants in controlled clinical trials for moderate depression. Interpersonal therapy, based on the social learning model of Harry Stack Sullivan (1953; Klerman, Weissman, Rounsaville, & Chevron, 1984), translates depressive symptoms into interpersonal issues. Typically these include the following situations: loss or grief issues, role transitions, role disputes, and intimacy problems. Each of these is a fruitful area to explore with clergy, nuns, and brothers. Although this model implies a cause–effect relationship with depression, a clinician may take a pragmatic approach toward alleviating depression no matter what its ultimate source.

ROLE DISPUTES

Role disputes are common for church personnel. As is evident from our previous descriptions, clerical life is a balancing act between various factions within the congregation. The more gifted the minister the more likely that pockets of conflict will develop. As noted in chapter 3 on anxiety disorders, the minister's innate interest in service to others results in a stance oriented toward mediating conflict and creating harmony.

What strikes the casual observer of the religious scene is the degree of diversity within a single congregation. Contrary to media stereotypes, most mainstream American religions have fundamentalist, conservative, and liberal subgroups within the same worshiping community. People join religious groups for idiosyncratic reasons ranging from sublime (theological consistency) to mundane (geographic convenience), so that heterogeneity is the rule not the exception.

Fundamentalists typically adhere literally to the beliefs and tenets of the faith community, whether that includes a literal belief in the Bible or complete obedience to authority. They tend to view deviation from these tenets as loss of salvation or at least sinful. Conservatives tend to maintain a close observance to the religious traditions, yet try to integrate their religious lives with positive values in their culture or advances in science and technology. Liberals tend to view their religious tradition as containing valuable insight into core concerns. Sacred writings and traditions for them are sources of wisdom not doctrines demanding internal assent.

To complicate matters further, these distinctions are fluid in practice so that a member may take a liberal position on one issue but a conservative one on others. Beliefs in religious groups are analogous to political viewpoints. Rare is the citizen who views every social issue through the lens of one political system. A believer may hold that the Virgin birth of Christ is literally true, but the idea of God creating the world in 7 days is a metaphor. Or, a believer may be conservative about creedal dogma but liberal about sexual ethics. To add to the confusion, ministers themselves will vary all across this spectrum. They may have learned the latest advances in biblical studies and archaeology in the seminary but dare not preach such notions from the pulpit. Although each congregation will have an evident majority from each of these positions, the minister is sure to bump against one or another of these other perspectives. When we realize that we have only described theological sources of dispute and have left out the ever-present personality sources, the wonder is that any minister can manage such disparity.

Common Sources of Role Disputes

The clinician may want to assess three common sources of role disputes. The first concerns authority. This refers either to immediate authority in the congregational structure (e.g., the pastor above you), or to the remote authority (bishop or regional authority).

The second concerns handling authority with staff. Religion professionals in management positions, such as pastors, often suffer from overinclusion. That is, they are committed to the religious ideals of their faith tradition and attempt to create, as far as humanly possible, a working environment that models those tenets. Overinclusion sets in, however, when they discover that staff members may not operate on the same principles, or that staff behavior is sabotaging the group's mission. The religious group may have difficulty accepting that other principles apply, such as laws regarding sexual harassment, due process, and complex labor law. The principles of secular organizations and law may conflict with the minister's attempt to resolve a situation using a treasured religious principle. The pastor becomes extremely discouraged and disheartened when she consults the Bible for guidance in a dispute but the staff member consults an attorney.

The third area involves handling disputes with the congregation at large. Often conflict arises over policy, e.g., to take on a new work of charity, to build a new worship area, to start a school. Congregations have high expectations of their leaders, not the least of which is expecting the minister to have excellent interpersonal skills for one-to-one counseling and excellent skills in managing large-group dynamics. This expectation is often unrealistic. Even trained clinicians do not always have superior skills in both individual and group therapy.

Therapy for Role Disputes

Strategies vary depending upon the circumstances, but we will address the three areas noted in broad terms. Authority role disputes often benefit from a combination of cognitive and role-playing interventions. At the cognitive level assessing the minister's expectations regarding the dispute with authority is beneficial. Ministers often have a host of expectations that, when strongly held, leave them feeling frustrated and unappreciated. These include, but are not limited to, the following:

1. Those in authority should be especially representative of religion's ideals (e.g., should be "Christlike").
2. Authority should take a personal interest in their well-being, growth, and development.
3. Authority should not use political means to accomplish its goals but means based on the group's religious tenets.
4. Authority should be supportive of them in any dispute they have with other groups.

Therapy might proceed by asking the client to self-monitor expectations about authority and evaluate carefully how closely expectations match the reality of the current situation. How reasonable is it for the bishop of a large urban diocese to express a personal interest in a young associate pastor? Can a religious group lack "politics" in its bureaucracy, in its selection of leaders, in deciding policy? Psychodynamic therapists may pursue these expectations along developmental lines from family of origin, while other approaches may be content with the cognitive insights alone. Once identified, the minister then challenges these expectations in standard cognitive therapy fashion.

Behavioral and interpersonal strategies rely on assertiveness training in handling disputes. Role-playing, behavioral rehearsal, empty-chair techniques, etc., are all possible ways to assess and develop skills in handling disputes. Given the potential for misunderstanding the cultural context of disputes, the therapist needs to get the cultural lay of the land. Therapists can accomplish this through discussion but also by having the client first role-play the authority figure. The role-playing will make clear subtleties such as the degree of familiarity permitted in the encounter.

Role disputes regarding staff members or work relationships may require the same interventions as those with authority. Additionally, however, seeking management consultation
may help the situation. To our knowledge religious professionals do not routinely attend courses on "Principles of Management for Religious Institutions," helpful though they would
be. The situation is so deficient that a group of energetic clergy,
vowed religious, and laity created a national organization for
church personnel (The National Association of Clergy and
Church Personnel). This organization shares with interested
groups documents regarding management laws and practice
for church settings, and holds an annual conference with practical workshops on church personnel issues.

Finding appropriate management consultation is not always easy. The therapist may be helpful, depending on his or
her experience. Larger church groups often provide consultation through their regional administration. Such consultation
is not available for smaller religious groups or those in which
the local congregation is autonomous. At times the only solution is for the client or congregation to purchase consultation
from management specialists. Here, again, the consultation will
only be valuable if the liaison understands the particular religious culture.

Role disputes involving groups within the congregation
expose a common deficiency in clergy training, namely group
dynamics. An overview of total ministry reveals the enormous
proportion of effort in group settings: organizational meetings,
planning committees, policy meetings, governing-body meetings, worship planning, groups for children, young adults, married couples, senior citizens, and prayer fellowship. Only an
extreme theology would expect God to suspend the principles
of human group behavior during gatherings of the faithful.
When we teach group therapy courses to graduate students in
pastoral counseling, many of whom are ordained clergy or
vowed religious, the universal response is, "Why do we not
have this course in seminary or formation?" When we present
workshops in coping with difficult people in congregations, we
see that the only way to address the effects of dysfunctional
group interaction is to change the group norms. When we

name the antidote we receive only blank stares. The methods for changing group norms are not available to them. They are unaware of even basic distinctions such as process and content.

Clients benefit from enrolling in a practical college course in group dynamics. It is a worthwhile investment in developing a sense of confidence in handling group situations. A useful course should teach concepts such as group norms, forming cohesiveness, how to run an efficient meeting, process vs. content, balancing group tasks with the personal needs of the members, and how to handle large group meetings. This may also be cost-effective and efficient in contrast to laboriously developing these skills through psychotherapy.

TRANSITION ISSUES

Interpersonal theory suggests that depression is correlated with role transition. Examples include beginning or ending a formal program of studies, transfer geographically within the same type of ministry, transfer into a totally new form of ministry, an assignment or election to administrative duties following direct pastoral care. The minister may not appreciate the immense satisfaction he or she derived from a job well done, and the large network of social contacts inherent in their work. Consequently, when reassigned, alienation or loneliness overwhelms the person. Each new assignment involves the tedious process of initiating and maintaining new social relationships and adjusting to work. Learning theory instructs us that depression results from loss of reinforcers. Any new assignment means the minister is without the satisfaction of former friends and available recreational pursuits. From finding a new jogging path to a favorite restaurant, pleasant events naturally decrease in new assignments. The large geographical boundaries that many ministers labor in ensure leaving behind much of what is satisfying with each transfer.

Often ministers handle the negative feelings through spiritual coping. Some tell themselves that their work is really God's work and human attachments interfere with the mission. The Christian minister recalls Jesus' words, "And everyone who has given up houses or brothers or sisters or father or mother or children or lands for the sake of my name will receive a hundred times more, and will inherit eternal life" (Matthew 19:29, *The New American Bible*, 1988). Through the defense mechanism Bowlby (1988) describes as excessive self-reliance, ministers numb themselves from grieving human attachments. Simultaneously the reality of adjusting to new assignments is an intricate and delicate process. A woman pastor, who was deeply loved by her congregation, transferred to a new church 60 miles away. A group from her former parish decided to "surprise" her by attending her maiden sermon at her new church. An associate pastor from the former church got wind of the plan and stopped it. She pointed out how awkward the pastor would feel simultaneously juggling expressing appreciation to her former congregants and paying attention to her new ones.

The natural inertia inherent to depression further impedes efficient bonding within the new social context. Activating the client to take small, essential steps toward relationship building is the clinical task. This includes accepting invitations to visit people, attending receptions, exploring the merchant and business community, investigating social organizations, finding recreational clubs and activities, obtaining a library card, or joining bible-study or prayer groups. In short, the person must put energy into any activity that has a reasonable probability of generating an active social life. Married ministers with dependent children have a built-in mechanism for social contacts. Children, as any introverted parent knows, are a ready-made window to the social environment. Natural groups involving school and child recreation serve this purpose well.

Transition is more complicated when replacing a distressed or impaired minister. The previous leader may have had a substance abuse problem, gambled excessively, misappropriated funds, engaged in sexual misconduct, or simply alienated many in the congregation by inept ministry or through an abrasive personality. The new minister may not experience the customary warmth and friendliness traditional with reassignment. The atmosphere is tense and the congregation's pain may manifest itself throughout a probationary period until trust develops. Following a beloved leader presents its own set of problems. Congregations often handle their loss by reminding the new leader just how wonderful Sister X was and how much they miss her. Even the most self-actualized person finds this tiresome and may wonder whether it is possible to establish an independent identity.

Some congregations or organizations are notorious for chewing up even skilled ministers. From a diagnostic viewpoint we would say that the organization is dysfunctional and persons with severe personality disorders are in control. Two styles of control typically develop in these situations. In one the group totally controls policy, process, and planning, reducing the leader to servitude. In the second, passive–aggressive interactive styles calcify the organization. Ministers going into such situations require the following strategies:

1. The total support of the regional authorities, whom the leader briefs at regular intervals.
2. Maintain strict boundaries initially between ministry-related and social–recreational relationships. Eventually the minister will have to confront the group's behavior, so emotional distance simplifies this.
3. Keep spouses and family members alert to the political intricacies so that they, too, can maintain appropriate boundaries.
4. Have an occupational escape route. Before accepting such assignments, the minister makes an agreement with superiors for an early reassessment (e.g., 6 months) to avoid locking into a long-term agreement.
5. As in other high stress situations, maintain a healthy lifestyle including an active recreational orientation and personal time.

These ingredients do not guarantee success but they are a safety net in case of failure.

INTIMACY ISSUES AND DEPRESSION

Lack of intimacy represents an important source of depression. Research demonstrates that for women intimacy provides the surest buffer against depression. In distressed marriages the rates of depression are 10 times higher than average for the population. A priest who counseled couples often mused, "There must be nothing more painful than going to sleep each night next to somebody you don't like."

Developing intimacy for clergy and vowed religious provides its own unique set of challenges. First a commitment to celibacy will limit how the minister chooses to express intimacy (cf. chapter 8). Others, for whom celibacy is not at issue, must decide to pursue relationships intended to result in marriage. They must address the role sexual expression will play in the relationship.

For the minister seeking marital intimacy the social context magnifies every step. Invariably the search must exclude persons with whom ministers have professional relationships (cf. chapter 9). This not only limits the field, but in a small town or rural area, lowers statistical probabilities to the level of state lotteries. The field shrinks further when limited to persons the minister is most likely to find attractive and be attractive to. Seeking out potential partners from highly dissimilar backgrounds increases the risk of a failed relationship.

For a healthy relationship both parties need to experience a sense of freedom, yet the fishbowl existence of ministry constrains both parties. Every choice the minister makes, including the person's name, level of involvement, joint activities, travel decisions, family backgrounds, and movie rentals become grist for the congregation's social mill.

In therapy the client weights each step from a cost–benefit perspective, not the most romantic basis to search for intimacy. For single women ministers the issues are even more intricate. Due to differing standards and perceptions of women's social behavior, she risks invoking the stigma of stereotype. Should she choose to behave in a way that is normative either for nonclergy women or male ministers, congregants may sanction her behavior. This creates fewer social opportunities to meet suitable partners possibly enhancing alienation in an already counterculture occupation.

For the celibate cleric or religious intimate nonsexual friendships remain essential as a buffer against depression.

Chapter 8 discusses in detail the intricacies of managing such relationships, so we will not discuss them here except to underline their importance as a buffer against depression. The same tasks face celibate and married religious professionals in role disputes or transition situations.

When a married minister is depressed, marital work is essential either as adjunctive treatment or as the primary modality. The family experiences a heavy burden required by the secrecy most ministers cherish. The family carries the secret with the minister sensing the condition's shame and they, too, have constraints from finding relief and support outside the family. Nor are they immune from the standard reactions of living with depressed persons. Research shows that after initial attempts to support a depressed person, friends and loved ones feel demoralized when the depressed person repeatedly rejects their attempts to reach out. Eventually they distance themselves inadvertently increasing the isolation of the client.

Family therapy can relieve some of this burden as members learn that their reactions are normal, that they did not cause the depression, and that the depressed person appreciates their positive support. Major components in the marital therapy of depression are:

1. Increasing the amount of positive reinforcement between partners; e.g., engaging in individually and mutually satisfying activities.
2. Developing basic communication skills such as reflective listening, mirroring, and empathy expression.
3. Implementing problem solving skills, so that the couple has a tool for navigating the inevitable conflicts in a close relationship.

5.

Guilt

GUILT AND COUNTERTRANSFERENCE

Religious guilt often generates puzzlement and helplessness in clinicians. Several barriers may contribute to therapist misunderstanding of guilt in ministers. First, cultural factors arise from the "religiosity gap" between clinicians and clients identified by Allen Bergin (1991). A survey of clinical psychologists found that 50% answered "none" to the question, "What religion are you?" This contrasts with nearly three-quarters of people in the United States stating that religion is either "very important" or "important" to them (Hoge, 1996).

Second, emotional guilt resists logic or rational evidence. Cognitive and rational-emotive therapies require considerable skill to make inroads on excessive religious guilt. At one point in his career Albert Ellis (1983) concluded that religion makes people neurotic. It is no simple task to argue someone out of their guilt and perhaps Ellis was responding to that frustration.

Equal resistance exists to behavioral strategies that require clients to act in ways perceived as violating important religious norms. If my client with obsessive–compulsive disorder believes that looking at an attractive woman is sinful through committing "adultery of the heart," I cannot simply prescribe exposure therapy and tell him to look at attractive models on television.

97

Furthermore, the cognitive schemas that are the source of excessive guilt often fall under the phenomenological category of overvalued ideas. Falling midway between irrational ideas and delusions, they have properties of each. In some instances they fall closer to one end of this spectrum than the other. Guilt triggered by religious belief tends to function as an over-valued idea. The person may have some appreciation of the senselessness of their overvalued ideas but often they hold a substantive truth-value. Consequently they are difficult to shake particularly when clients believe their immortal souls are at stake.

Finally, clinicians may misunderstand the categories used by religious persons to distinguish dimensions of guilt. Many therapists, starting with Freud, subsume conscience under the category of emotion. In this framework guilt is a feeling associated with a real or imagined transgression in the moral order. Freud made precise speculations regarding the origin of this faculty.

Students of theology or ethics, however, distinguish at least two aspects of conscience. The first is the psychological under-standing of guilt as an emotion arising from violating one's conscience. The second is the philosophical–theological under-standing of conscience as a moral *judgment,* an act of the intellect determining the rightness or wrongness of an act. Guilt, in this sense, may or may not be connected to a negative emotional feeling. Essentially it describes a moral *condition,* similar to the legal understanding of the terms *guilt* and *innocence.* Guilt, therefore, may result from conscience in either the psychological or theological sense.

Misunderstanding between client and therapist may easily arise from equivocal use of the terms *conscience* and *guilt.* Therapists are prone to see conscience and guilt in negative terms, while ministers, as students of moral behavior, are prone to see them as dynamic positive activities that lead us to the good. As an example of differences in approaching these categories, in 1971 the American Psychological Association invited philosopher of religion Walter Kaufmann to speak at its annual convention on topics later discussed in his book *Without Guilt or Justice* (1973). Kaufmann's position that guilt is essentially a destructive and unnecessary emotion was well received by participants, a position antithetical to many religious believers.

Countertransference issues related to guilt may also play out through personality differences between client and therapist. Religious or nonreligious persons who are guilt-prone tend to have personality traits that personality tests describe as rigid or closed. In the five-factor model of personality, for example, they are likely to think in black-or-white cognitive categories, prefer absolute answers, and be closed to new ideas. This style is problematic in psychotherapy on at least two counts. First, these qualities relate to a poor response to psychotherapy in general, when psychotherapy is defined as insight or psychodynamically oriented approaches. Second, such persons are often closed to behavioral strategies that trigger conflict with their traditional values or worldview. When Masters and Johnson (1970) analyzed their treatment failures in sex therapy, the one variable that consistently correlated was strong orthodox religious beliefs, i.e., conservative Catholicism, fundamental Protestantism, or orthodox Judaism. Therapists, on the other hand, typically possess personality styles that are open and they highly value flexible ways of thinking. This sets the stage for therapists to perceive such clients as narrow-minded obscurantists and for clients to view therapists as ethical relativists.

Finally, countertransference issues can emerge in the guise of ethical dilemmas between client and therapist. Questions related to moral guilt sometimes raise ethical issues for therapists that are atypical to the standard ones that arise in psychotherapy. In the usual scenario therapists refuse to cooperate in a client's expressed behavior, e.g., wanting to physically harm self or others. With religious clients therapists may have difficulty condoning morally *restrained* behavior.

A seminarian seeks treatment in a university counseling center. The overt behavioral symptom he wishes to work on is what he terms excessive masturbation. The counselor-trainee assesses the problem to discover that the client would be satisfied with masturbating "once or twice a month," but is uncomfortable with his current regimen of four to five times a week. The trainee discusses this case in his group supervision. The team,

in agreement with the clinical supervisor, conclude that masturbation here is merely a symptom of underlying psychic conflict.
The trainee suggests to the client that they work on "deeper"
issues, and that ethically the counselor could not make reducing
the frequency of masturbation a primary treatment goal. Because the client insisted on reducing masturbation, the counselor referred him to a behaviorally oriented therapist who was
willing to treat it as a primary problem.

Examples such as this affirm the complexities of the culture
gap between some psychological models and the goals of religious persons.

COPING WITH MORAL GUILT

Once the therapist determines that moral guilt relates to the
client's distress, two approaches are helpful. The first, and one
that often works with laypersons as well, is to suggest adjunctive
religious counseling or spiritual direction. All major religions
have a refined conceptualization of forgiveness related to personal guilt. Referral to a sensible religious counselor, who generates confidence in the client, alleviates the need for the
therapist either to acquire or act as surrogate for the spiritual
dimension.

Referrals, however, need to respect the value of spiritual
direction or religious counseling as a profession. We have observed mental health professionals fail to respect pastoral or
religious counselors in at least two ways. One is to simply avoid
the traditional consultation–liaison model that is standard practice between health care providers. No therapist would even
consider referring a client to a psychiatrist for medication evaluation without discussing the case with the psychiatrist. Yet, in
our experience, not consulting with the religious counselor is
the norm. The second respect issue is a condescending tone
when consultation does occur. Although education varies
greatly among religious denominations, most clergy and vowed
religious have graduate degrees, and many have taken courses
in mental health or abnormal psychology. One can assume that
the average religious counselor will have sufficient familiarity

with mental health concepts and terminology to comprehend the therapist's treatment plan. In the case of pastoral counselors, this assumption is even more accurate. For example, the graduate program in which we teach requires more clinical and theory courses than secular counseling programs. Our program, as is the case for most university affiliated pastoral counseling programs, maintains accreditation from the nationally recognized counseling boards. Graduates are eligible for licensing or certification as counselors in their states. Therefore, to either avoid or treat religious counselors condescendingly is both bad business and violates most professional ethical codes regarding relationships with other disciplines. More importantly these practices jeopardize client welfare by creating a potential conflict for the client who has to integrate advice from persons with different viewpoints.

Many clergy and vowed religious, however, do not require separate referral. They will have sufficient education in their own theological traditions to cope with moral guilt, if only they could access their spiritual repertoire. What they require is guidance to attend to that repertoire. Using a cognitive model the therapist can ask the client to self-monitor guilt-inducing cognitions. As they record upsetting thoughts the therapist evokes from them spiritual resources, theological themes, or statements from Scripture or other religious writing that counteract or challenge the guilt associated with their negative thinking. The client also records these spiritual "challenges" to use at a later time in the case of relapse.

Clinicians from many therapy traditions agree on the importance of client metaphors. The cognitive model outlined here is also analogous to a metaphor. One client can reason through in cognitive or rational-emotive style the theological underpinnings of forgiveness and receive comfort. Another client will accomplish the same thing through the use of a metaphor such as the image of Jesus as the Good Shepherd who leaves 99 "saved" sheep to look for the one that is lost. The caution here is for therapist flexibility. Linear thinking in syllogistic form may help some clients, but in the area of spirituality metaphors may have more "cognitive" power to influence negative emotions. We as therapists are culture-bound to our personal religious or spiritual metaphors. We can, however, through attentive listening and empathy evoke the client's metaphor of healing and forgiveness.

TREATMENT OF EMOTIONAL GUILT

Therapists can approach some forms of emotional guilt in a similar manner from a cognitive framework. The logic remains the same as in the form for moral guilt. The only difference is that, in addition to the spiritual challenges (or restructuring), the therapist should feel free to evoke a variety of dimensions that counteract the guilt-inducing thoughts. For example, Pastor Alice feels guilty for taking time away from her family to attend to parishioner needs. In addition to using her spiritual metaphors to challenge her negative beliefs she also notes the significant time and energy she does put into family life.

A second form of emotional guilt also exists within religious persons that more closely resembles what is familiar to clinicians as arising from an obsessive–compulsive disorder. This condition has a long history within the field of applied spiritual care and moral theologians labeled the condition *scrupulosity*. Readers interested in an in-depth look at the historical, clinical, and treatment dimensions of this condition might consult *The Doubting Disease: Help for Scrupulosity and Religious Compulsions* (Ciarrocchi, 1995a). The condition affected many historically important religious persons, either as a chronic condition or for prolonged periods. They include Martin Luther, John Bunyan, and Saint Ignatius Loyola, founder of the Jesuits.

Although the condition known as obsessive–compulsive disorder (OCD) has many variations, its religious manifestation is to see sin where there is none. The cultural implications involved in assessing this form are apparent from the definition. First, it requires the clinician to understand what constitutes sin from the client's perspective. Second, the clinician must judge that the client's interpretation of sin is scrupulous in this instance; that is, the client is seeing sin where there is none. To make that determination the clinician must have the prerequisite understanding of the client's religious–moral tradition to provide the background context for the client's symptom. Clinicians, therefore, may require consultation from religious experts to complete their assessment. Is it really a violation of the Sunday work laws for this person to plant tulip bulbs in her garden? Must this couple abstain from sex during the menstrual period? Does eating vegetable soup made with clear chicken broth violate a meatless dietary restriction?

Clinicians may know the answer to these questions only when clients come from their own religious tradition. But, as noted above, in many cases clinicians do not belong to any religious institution, or, if they do, may not be familiar with their client's tradition. By temperament clinicians are not fond of legalisms. Persons with OCD have a black-or-white mentality with regard to their symptoms. They crave absolute answers on questions of moral doubt. Clinicians usually have a high tolerance for ambiguity something foreign to someone in the grip of OCD. It requires a great deal of energy and going against the grain for the clinician to research the minutiae of religious moral codes, and still greater energy to remain sympathetic with persons who obsess about them. A further countertransference issue is to take the view of "a pox on both your houses," meaning that clinicians may lose patience with both clients and their religious institutions. An easy trap to fall in is to blame the institution for creating OCD in the person. Just as we have moved away from concepts such as the "schizophrenogenic" mother, no simple environment–pathology link exists for OCD.

Scrupulosity even takes on a developmental feature in the lives of deeply religious persons thus requiring even greater understanding from clinicians. Two examples of developmental scrupulosity exist but only one concerns us here. The first is the form taken during adolescence. Some young people, usually in early adolescence, go through a phase of exquisite moral sensitivity. They seek reassurance about their own moral behavior or that of family and friends. The pattern has the hallmarks of OCD but usually is transitory and remits with patient advice and adult guidance.

The form clinicians may face in therapy with religious professionals is the type that occurs after some profound religious conversion or experience. Many revered saints went through phases of scrupulosity, seeing evil where most would not. Saint Ignatius of Loyola, for example, went through a period when he would constantly watch his feet when walking to avoid stepping on two pieces of straw or grass in the shape of a cross, lest he commit blasphemy. This form, too, usually remits in time with appropriate guidance. The strategies we suggest below for OCD-related scrupulosity are applicable to developmental scrupulosity as well.

Religious persons with OCD complicate clinical assessment because they often hide their symptoms feeling ashamed of the eccentric behavior OCD generates. They worry, further, that a secular therapist will either misunderstand or even ridicule the religious dimensions of their symptoms. Most people with the disorder recognize the irrational nature of their symptoms and presume others will react accordingly. Associated with this is the fear that the therapist assumes that the *cause* of the symptoms is the person's religion and will influence the person to abandon religion in order to restore health. Some worry, also, that the treatment plan will suggest strategies that are morally unacceptable.

> Bill, a Baptist pastor, obsessed over whether or not he had actually "committed adultery in his heart" with an attractive woman he noticed. The therapist, after many futile attempts to uncover the "deeper meaning" of this obsession, suggested that perhaps the client really was unhappy in his marriage and wanted to have an affair.

Horrified at this interpretation, Bill ended treatment. Similarly, in the area of sexual guilt therapists sometimes recommend masturbation to religious clients. We generally hear from clients how this strategy backfires, since rarely do clients comply, or if they do, the guilt associated with the behavior becomes a new symptom expression.

ASSESSMENT OF SCRUPULOSITY

A practical strategy in assessing the religious symptoms of OCD is to delineate obsessions from compulsions. The distinction within the DSM-IV (American Psychiatric Association, 1994), which has long been the criterion for behavior therapy, is most useful. Simply put, obsessions are anxiogenic; they trigger anxiety and take the form of ideas, urges, feelings, impulses or acts. Clinicians well know the traditional obsessions and we will not dwell on them here (e.g., my hands are contaminated). Compulsions are anxiolytic; they are repetitive acts in response to obsessions and function to reduce anxiety (e.g., hand washing to purify from contamination). Typical religious obsessions include concerns that one has committed any of the following irreligious or immoral acts: blasphemy; aggression toward another; sexual misdeeds in the form of illicit acts, ideas, or feelings; or the violation of some religious ritual. Religious compulsions are the presumed antidote to the religious obsession. They may take the form of the following: repeated prayers to expiate one's misdeeds, repeating a religious practice or ritual because of uncertainty that it was done exactly (e.g., ritual washing, confession), avoiding looking at attractive persons lest one be "tempted," or seeking repeated reassurance from others regarding their safety. Some period of self-monitoring obsessions and compulsions is crucial. Many excellent self-help and therapy manual guides for the treatment of OCD have recording forms for this purpose and are noted in the References and Suggested Readings Section.

> Reverend Schultz, of the Assembly of God, has ceased interacting with his family, spending all available time consumed in biblical study and conversations with biblical scholars at local theological schools. His [then] hero, Reverend Jimmy Swaggart, sermonized on videotape about the "unpardonable sin against the Holy Ghost," described in the Gospel of Matthew. According to Jesus' words, all sins can be forgiven except this one. Since hearing this sermon, determining whether he did or did not commit this sin has preoccupied him. Although the biblical passage is quite vague and scholars do not agree regarding what

sin Jesus refers to, Reverend Schultz drives himself to find an answer. He consults every reference work available on the topic from interlibrary loan and besieges scholars who are capable of reading the original Greek texts to enlighten him. Although he is unable to obtain a satisfactory explanation of what the sin is, nevertheless he feels quite strongly that he has committed it.

In this example the obsession is the idea or belief that one may have committed the "unpardonable" sin. It is intrusive and senseless to the degree that even the most learned in the faith community have no absolute answer. The compulsion is the frantic search to identify what the sin is so that he can gain assurance about his personal responsibility. John Bunyan recorded this same obsession that still haunts OCD sufferers in *Grace Abounding* (1666/1988) three centuries ago. Persons with OCD who emphasize a literal interpretation of the Bible are susceptible to this obsession. The example illustrates the importance of religious or theological consultation for the therapist. This obsession could confuse even therapists who are Christian unless they were familiar with evangelical Christianity. The therapist must assess each obsessive–compulsive symptom similarly, breaking it down in terms of anxiogenic or anxiolytic functions before behavioral treatment can go forward.

BEHAVIORAL TREATMENT OF SCRUPULOSITY

We assume that the most effective psychological treatment strategy for scrupulosity is a behavioral model with certain modifications. Insight-oriented treatment is largely ineffective and the behavioral treatment described here constitutes an empirically validated treatment. We will, however, describe in detail the necessary modification of behavioral treatment for religious professionals, but at the same time adhere to a recognizable behavioral approach.

To date, the most effective behavioral strategy for OCD is combining exposure to the anxiety-eliciting obsessions while at the same time preventing the performance of the anxiety-reducing compulsions. In the classic pattern clients with hand-washing rituals are exposed to water taps but taught to tolerate the anxiety that comes with not washing. The same model works with scrupulosity but the mental nature of many religious obsessions and compulsions requires considerable effort and vigilance.

The first step is to share with clients the symptom structure of their obsessions and compulsions. Figure 5.1 provides one illustration of such a model. The advantage to proceeding in this manner is that intelligent clients often anticipate the logic of the therapeutic interventions. They readily see that the compulsion serves to reinforce the obsession and that logically the compulsion must cease if they are to gain control over the obsession.

The next step is to outline the exposure and response prevention strategy symptom by symptom. If the client has followed your explanation of the function of obsessions and compulsions, the next step is obvious. The example of a child throwing a temper tantrum in the candy aisle of the grocery store can make this point. If dad buys candy for his daughter when she whines in a low voice, low whining will get the candy each time. If dad now tries to set limits and refuses to buy the candy, the daughter will typically escalate. If dad buys it now, Suzie will probably scream the next time, with dad and Suzie caught in a never-ending spiral of dad refusing, Suzie escalating, dad giving in. Asking clients how to stop the spiral usually brings the response, "Dad has to say, 'No,' and hold his ears." This commonsense understanding of behavioral extinction is the groundwork for exposure and response prevention. Using Figure 5.1 the therapist makes the same point. To eliminate the obsession with the unpardonable sin the client has to cease reinforcing it through his endless search for reassurance.

At this point treatment resistance often occurs. Aside from natural reluctance to engage in an anxiety-provoking act, client resistance with scrupulosity treatment often results from overvalued ideas. A clinical understanding of overvalued ideas appreciates how they stand midway between rational and delusional thinking. Overvalued ideas drive religious compulsions because the stakes are high for clients. The consequences of not checking a water tap before bedtime does not compare with the consequences of committing an act that, for believers,

Figure 5.1
Model for Development of Scrupulosity

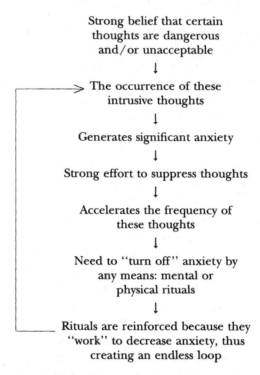

Strong belief that certain
thoughts are dangerous
and/or unacceptable
↓
The occurrence of these
intrusive thoughts
↓
Generates significant anxiety
↓
Strong effort to suppress thoughts
↓
Accelerates the frequency of
these thoughts
↓
Need to "turn off" anxiety by
any means: mental or
physical rituals
↓
Rituals are reinforced because they
"work" to decrease anxiety, thus
creating an endless loop

Source: From *The Doubting Disease*, by J. W. Ciarrocchi (p. 28). Copyright © 1995 by J. W. Ciarrocchi. Reprinted by permission of Paulist Press.

affects the immortal state of their souls. Sometimes clients sardonically ask the therapist, "If I comply with treatment, will you be present when I die to explain your strategy to my Maker?"

Given this presumed personal cost, an effective strategy to overcome this resistance is to collaborate with a religious advisor. Imagine you are treating Sister Catherine, whose chore is to sweep the carpet in the church sanctuary. Imagine, further, that she is compulsive about not vacuuming any area that has small specks of white fearing they are remnants from Holy Communion. The standard behavioral strategy in this case would be to encourage her to vacuum everything, perhaps rapidly, but guiding her to not give in to the compulsion of picking up every speck, putting it in a water glass, and pouring it down the special sink for disposing of Communion remains. You may or may not understand the religious practice involved in her symptoms but a power struggle over the strategy is highly likely. It could lead to an endless discussion of dogma and her spending much energy to make sure you understand her "position." An alternative is to refer her to a religious advisor with the following question. "I am seeing a therapist to help me with my scrupulosity, and Dr. Jones suggests that I might do the following. . . . Dr. Jones wants to know whether I am permitted to do this?" Have the client seek guidance for each strategy; some may be permissible, some not. As a result, the client has both a supply of intervention strategies as well as the necessary religious approval.

From this point standard exposure and response prevention is the psychological treatment of choice. Clinicians familiar with this treatment for OCD realize the subtlety of creating exposure strategies. When both obsessions and compulsions are mental acts, discovering appropriate strategies requires enormous creativity. For example, what is the strategy for a man whose compulsion is to say a brief prayer whenever he feels "tempted" by noticing an attractive woman? Response prevention implies simply not praying. But, if the base rate for the behavior is intermittent and occurs only in crowded areas, the opportunity to prevent the response is too infrequent to be effective. To provide an opportunity for response prevention requires the person to place himself in situations where the compulsive urge is strong.

Table 5.1 is a recording sheet that also gives the basic exposure and response prevention strategies in capsule form to the client. Clients easily get confused as to whether they approach or avoid certain urges. We have simplified this with St. Ignatius' dictum of "Do the opposite" of the impulse. If the impulse is to do something, avoid it. If it is to avoid something, then do it. We have found this less confusing than having to explain the distinctions between exposure and response prevention and which symptoms get treated by which strategy.

The therapist must gain the client's acceptance to such a strategy, perhaps taking walks during lunch in an urban business district, or viewing attractive models in a magazine. Purely

TABLE 5.1
Worksheet for Changing Compulsions
Day/Date

Exposure Strategy:	Compulsion:	Guidelines:
Think about or place yourself in situations that trigger disturbing thought, impulse, image or ritual.	Thought, image, impulse, or act that reduces anxiety.	1) Stay in situation until tension level drops to mild range.
	Blocking Strategy: Do the Opposite.	Scale
	1) If impulse to avoid object or activity—DO IT.	1 = No anxiety
Describe situation or thought.	2) If impulse to do something: e.g. repeat, check, pray, seek reassurance—prevent the response.	2–3 = Mild anxiety 4–5 = Moderate anxiety 6–7 = Severe anxiety 8–10 = Intense anxiety
	Initial Tension Level 1–10 Amount of time spent exposed to situation Final Tension Level 1–10	2) If anxiety becomes intense, consider "reporter" strategy while staying in situation.

Source: From *The Doubting Disease*, by J. W. Ciarrocchi (p. 90). Copyright © 1995 by J. W. Ciarrocchi. Reprinted by permission of Paulist Press.

mental obsessions and compulsions are the most difficult for clients to gain control over and many religious symptoms are only mental.

Medication, of course, is an alternative or adjunctive treatment for OCD. In our experience, however, clients with scrupulosity have strong resistance to medication. Perhaps it stems from the hypochondriasis commonly associated with OCD. At any rate, rational persuasion is not an effective tactic with this condition. For those who take medication behavioral strategies are a useful adjunct.

Developing ease with behavioral interventions for religious OCD enhances therapist effectiveness for subclinical scrupulosity as well. The emotional guilt we have described need not be related to full-blown OCD. Many religious professionals succumb to the effects of emotional guilt solely from learning experiences with intensely self-critical belief systems. The compulsive, driven individuals who exhibit either the popularly termed type A personality, or the clinical condition known as obsessive–compulsive personality disorder (OCPD), are also candidates for these strategies.

Reverend Ida is pastor of a large congregation with several associate pastors, a staff of religious educators, youth ministers, as well as several community outreach programs. Her efficient, task-oriented style has contributed both to her success and her chronic gastrointestinal upset. You assess that one of her characteristic stress patterns results from a fierce sense of time-urgency. Any perception that time is wasting increases her anxiety as well as her gastric secretions. You prescribe some standard behavioral tasks such as purposely standing in the longest checkout line at the supermarket. She complies with these simple strategies but has more difficulty when you work on a variety of "nondoing" exercises. She shares her tendency to see quiet time as alien to what she describes as her belief in the social Gospel, namely that we help Jesus when we help those in need. Further, in her mind, that is where and how we encounter God. You ask her to consult a respected spiritual guide of her faith. This advisor helps her reflect on what she really believes about the concept of grace. In reality she acts as if she believes that she has to do all the work, that God is merely a silent witness. Having absorbed this challenge, she returns to you and more readily enters into response prevention strategies, such as turning on the telephone answering machine for select periods each day.

In this way, exposure and response prevention become part of a clinical armamentarium for disparate self-defeating anxiety-coping responses.

PART III

Compulsive Behavior and Sexual Issues

In this section we take up problems associated with substance abuse, gambling, sexual problems, and celibacy. Some psychologists view many human problems as stemming from failure to self-regulate personal behavior (e.g., Baumeister, Heatherton, & Tice, 1994). Certainly this feature accounts for considerable problems in ministry as well, and here we discuss their typical range and contexts. In addition we provide a number of treatment guidelines for ministers with these problems.

6.

Addictive Disorders, Substance Use, and Gambling Disorders

In this chapter we will address addiction to alcohol and other drugs as well as gambling disorders. We discuss sexual problems separately in the next chapter. Difficulties with intervening in both disorders are similar, however, so that the material included here is relevant for engaging clients who have sexual problems. The topics covered in this chapter include cultural issues that feed denial, intervention strategies, and treatment strategies with an emphasis on coordinating with Twelve-Step programs.

INTERVENTION

Intervention refers to the process of engaging the client's commitment to changing maladaptive use of alcohol or other drugs. Clinicians are usually familiar with intervention that has its roots in the industrial model. Vernon Johnson (1980), alcohol specialist and Episcopalian priest, popularized this model through his training institute for alcoholism counselors which produced films detailing intervention steps. When former First Lady, Betty Ford, went public with her story of recovery from drug addiction, she described her personal intervention. A made-for-television movie of her recovery further popularized the steps taken by her family in its intervention with her.

The industrial–organizational model of intervention inspired this approach through use of natural contingencies in the work setting. In its essence an employer said to an impaired worker, "Get help or your fired." Rates of compliance with treatment and eventual recovery significantly increased over the ordinary methods of voluntary treatment or rational persuasion. Addiction counselors, then, adapted this model to embrace intervention with family members or friends even when no leverage was available from the work site. Most addiction specialists would consider this model as the standard intervention method in the field today.

Recently, however, some specialists have challenged this model as the most suitable for motivating clients into treatment. Psychologist William Miller (Miller & Rollnick, 1991), arguing from a conceptual framework that views recovery as involving various stages, maintains that confrontational models of intervention are too likely to generate resistance. Social psychology refers to this as "reactance," or the attempts an individual makes to maximize autonomy. Miller proposed an alternative model that emphasizes cognitive dissonance strategies. In this approach an interventionist presents diverse sets of information to the client, e.g., medical laboratory tests, neurocognitive functioning tests, legal data, or observations from friends, families, or employers. At the same time the specialist asks the client to reflect on the meaning of all this information in light of the client's partial belief that everything is fine. Miller's method is too subtle and clinically nuanced to present here in total but his model is a persuasive alternative. The National Institute of Alcoholism and Alcohol Abuse is currently overseeing a large treatment outcome study of alcoholism with this motivational interviewing technique as one condition under investigation. Results from the first year outcome reveal that as few as four sessions of motivational interviewing was as effective in reducing problem drinking as 12 sessions of more intensive group or cognitive–behavioral counseling (Project Match Research Group, 1997).

The clinician may resort to our conclusions, which is to combine both approaches for achieving compliance with treatment for clergy and vowed religious. Each model may have its usefulness depending upon the client's circumstances. The industrial–organizational model has merit in the cultural context of a resistant, impaired religious professional for whom the alternative to treatment is removal from his or her job, while motivational interviewing may have greater utility for the self-referred but ambivalent client. To assist the clinician in determining the appropriate approach we need first to examine the cultural context of addiction for religious professionals.

CULTURAL CONTEXT OF INTERVENTION

To fully appreciate the dynamics of intervention requires an understanding of the culture of authority that exists for clients. Authority structures in institutional religion take many shapes. Assessing the client's individual authority structure is most crucial when evaluating addictive behavior.

> A member of Sister Alice's residence calls to express concern about her erratic behavior that the community believes is linked to substance abuse. Until now they have only spoken with her in general terms, e.g., telling her they are concerned about her health, asking if she is all right, offering to help, inquiring whether she is under stress, etc. You hold a meeting with the five sisters who live with her and her regional superior, Sister Audrey. The sisters with sincere concern and personal pain eloquently describe the anguish of watching someone they care about deteriorate before their eyes.

The industrial–organizational model views this setting as analogous to that between a supervisor and employee. Although in this case the supervisor does not have control over Sister Alice's paycheck, the superior can make appeal to her organizational authority and order Sister Alice into treatment via the vow of obedience. Assuming the superior is willing to do this, the clinical task is to prepare each of the participants to write down a list of behaviors they have observed indicating impairment in Sister Alice and how this has affected them.

When each participant is ready the group arranges a meeting with Sister Alice. At the meeting each member shares her observations and at the end Sister Alice has an opportunity to respond. Following this model to its completion, the superior will first invite Sister Alice to seek evaluation and/or treatment for the problems described. In the according-to-script formula Sister Alice accepts these expressions of concern and agrees to seek help.

In reality, however, multiple scenarios develop. In one scenario the community members will not participate. In one case six community members refused to sit through such a confrontation and every one chose instead to move out of the residence, even though all were very happy with its location and amenities. In another scenario the superior refused to force the member into treatment. After the clinician prepared the community members for an intervention, the superior stated that his understanding of the vow of obedience was a collaborative one, and he could invite the member to seek treatment but could not order him to do so.

These examples should alert clinicians that even apparently monolithic church organizations can have a surprising degree of diversity that requires clinical acumen to adapt treatment models. A striking example of this occurred in a New England town when an associate bishop, contrary to professional advice, tried to persuade a pastor with a severe drinking problem to enter treatment. The "confrontation" took place when the bishop "just happened to be in the neighborhood," and encountered the pastor who was outside watering the rectory lawn. The bishop's attempt to get the pastor to enter treatment was met with stony silence and just the slightest suggestion that the water hose might shortly go out of control.

In Roman Catholic and similarly structured hierarchical religious organizations gaining the superior's cooperation is often the surest route to effective intervention. Although infrequently utilized, sanctions for direct disobedience exist. A superior who is willing to enforce his or her authority is usually successful in gaining treatment compliance. In many instances the most effective leverage relates to the client's ministerial job. Even in advanced stages of addiction religious professionals cling to their ministry for their last drops of self-esteem. If a religious superior does not have any leverage over the particular job of a member, the clinician will have to gain the cooperation of an immediate supervisor, perhaps by having the superior make contact with this individual. In decentralized organizations the local community or church will have to function both as employer and family if intervention is to succeed. For example, where local churches are autonomous, as is the case in some Protestant congregations, the church board or vestry will need to participate in motivating reluctant ministers. In any event, questioning continued employment is often the key motivational ingredient to obtaining compliance with evaluation or treatment. Keeping the vast cultural differences in mind the following outline provides a guideline for intervention.

Preparation

Intervention requires adequate preparation of all parties—superiors, colleagues, family, friends, and therapist. Obtaining concrete data is the crucial first step. Since the intervention is not a court of law, formal rules of evidence do not apply and participants' subjective reactions to their experiences with the client are critical data in the motivation process. For example, how the client's inconsistent mood swings makes others feel is of equal importance to the mood swings themselves. The personal, subjective pain that the client causes others is often the most powerful evidence of a need for intervention. Participants should write out their experiences emphasizing two points: (1) behavioral observations of the client; and (2) how the behavior affected them personally in terms of their thinking, feeling, and behavior.

What impedes intervention in some cases is the lack of a "smoking gun." Clergy and vowed religious, even in advanced stages of substance abuse, can hide its effects through a lifestyle that incorporates substantial periods out of public view. They can hold it together for public functions and disappear into alcoholic solitude. This may occur on days off or commonly in nightly drinking that is largely hidden. Persons who are polyaddicted to legal or illegal drugs are even more effective in masking outward signs of drug dependence.

To circumvent this absence of definitive data a helpful alternative is for the relevant community to conduct an intervention whose goal is *evaluation* for treatment, rather than a blanket endorsement of treatment itself. Here the participants can simply say, "Look, we are not experts in this field. All we know is that something is terribly wrong, that your behavior is affecting so many of us, and you seem to be hurting as well. We insist that you talk to experts and receive an evaluation; and when that's completed we can discuss the future." The advantage here is that no participant has to feel like "the bad guy" and label the person's behavior as addicted, alcoholic, or disturbed. The mental health professional plays that role. Furthermore, the professional will have access to data not available to superiors or peers, e.g., medical laboratory tests, clinical interviews, psychological testing, etc.

Clinical Assessment

In some instances the individual clinician may have the skills and assessment materials to provide the necessary evaluation. One option, however, is to employ addiction specialists to conduct the evaluation and provide the results. One model requires an interdisciplinary team with medical, psychosocial, and addiction specialists. Appropriate medical evaluation investigates health-related problems linked to substance abuse, including blood tests, physical examinations, and brain-imaging procedures. Neuropsychological tests are particularly sensitive to certain forms of chronic substance use, e.g., alcoholism. Brain impairment, in our experience, often creates powerful incentives for this educated population to enter treatment. Psychosocial evaluation by clinical social workers, psychologists, and other mental health specialists reviews the client's adaptive functioning for instances of impairment due to substance use. Effective psychosocial evaluation requires client consent to interview significant colleagues, family, supervisors and friends.

These collateral contacts often supply the missing pieces for clinical puzzles that are suggestive but lack hard evidence. Pastoral counselors assess the clients' spiritual integration to determine what emphasis clients place on spiritual growth in their daily lives. A common phenomenon with impaired clergy and religious is that their spiritual life is arid, and they have neglected it for many years. Religious professionals with addiction problems continue to function in the public sphere of religious life but have abandoned personal spiritual development. They neglect spiritual practices such as private personal prayer, regular meditation, growth-oriented spiritual reading, or participating in spiritual direction.

The information provided in the following tables summarizes clinical characteristics of patients referred for substance abuse evaluation and highlights typical findings for this group. Table 6.1 describes age, years of abuse, and IQ scores for a sample of 60 Roman Catholic clergy and sisters (48 men, 12 women), who represented consecutive admissions for an 18-month period in a 4-day evaluation program. Length of abuse ranged from 5 to 40 years highlighting the chronicity of the problem for many. The age percentages also show that substance abuse is a problem for both the young and old with 10% under 40 years old and 28% over 60. Perhaps more surprising is that a full 10% were over 70 years old highlighting the need to be conscious of alcoholism in the elderly and retired. As expected, these clients are above average on language-related IQ measures but performance IQ is notably lower, a finding that is correlated with cognitive impairment associated with acute alcoholism. Medical characteristics described in Table 6.2 are revealing. Four out of five had a medical condition related to alcohol use detectable by physical exam or laboratory test. Nearly 4 out of 10 (38%) had identifiable CT brain scan abnormalities. Related to this finding is the neuropsychological impairment found in over half of the clients.

Psychosocial characteristics, also in Table 6.2, indicate that over 90% were involuntary referrals, meaning that they came at the urging of their religious authorities rather than on their own. The rates of mixed substance abuse (11%) are lower than rates typically found in the general population of alcoholics in

TABLE 6.1
Age, Years of Abuse, and IQ Values for Chemically Dependent
Religious Professionals

	Mean	Range
Age	53	28–79
Years of Abuse	13	5–40
WAIS-R IQ Values		
Verbal IQ	112	84–138
Performance IQ	99	74–132

TABLE 6.2
Medical and Psychosocial Characteristics

Problem Area	Percentage
Alcohol-Related Medical Condition	82
Abnormal CT Brain Scan	38
Abnormal EEG	3
Mixed Substance Abuse	11
Familial Alcoholism	67
Involuntary Referral	92
Neuropsychological Impairment (Halstead-Reitan Battery)	
Total Score Impairment	54
Cognitive Flexibility	33
Nonverbal Abstraction	59
Sensory–spatial Problem Solving	52
Incidental Memory	67

treatment. This is not surprising given the enormous social stigma for drug use in such a high-status social group. Familial alcoholism, defined as heavy drinking in either parent, is 67%. This has significant clinical implications suggesting that, upon eventual recovery, developmental issues related to growing up in an alcoholic household will need addressing.

In a comprehensive evaluation program the team meets with the client along with a representative from the religious organization, e.g., a personnel director or religious superior. In the meeting the team presents the pertinent data along with diagnostic conclusions and recommendations. The client is invited to respond as is the representative. The community and the client then determine the next course of action, whether involving residential treatment, self-help group participation, outpatient therapy, etc.

Larger Protestant denominations, as well, have centrally organized policies and procedures for assisting ministers impaired by substance abuse. Often a substance abuse specialist works within the central office and functions as a liaison with the local church. The therapist who is preparing significant others for an intervention needs to inquire about the existence of such a specialist and contact them concerning available services.

With married ministers spouse and family involvement are essential for assessment and treatment. Although the approach is the same as with lay couples, the ministerial culture adds considerable complexity. Family members may or may not desire the assistance of church members in the intervention or support process. Sometimes the openness of the congregation is awe-inspiring in providing a totally supportive and welcoming atmosphere. Some lovingly encourage their ministers to seek help and welcome him or her following treatment. In other situations family members desire to maintain official silence with the congregation about the problem. The range of these options requires the therapists to assess the needs of the client carefully in relationship to the merits or problems with self-disclosure to the congregation.

Intervention Outcome

Many outcomes are possible after an intervention no matter what form it takes. Generally, the client, encouraged by the community, complies with treatment recommendations. On occasion clients will reject them. This leaves the community in a quandary, both practically and psychologically. For this reason a consulting relationship with the community for debriefing purposes provides a genuine service. Community members have placed themselves at considerable emotional risk by honestly demonstrating their care for the identified members, and now have to live with unfulfilled hopes. In addition they may feel awkward continuing a relationship that harbors resentment on both sides. One or two debriefing sessions with community members is useful whether or not the intervention leads to a treatment outcome. We have seen clients remain hostile toward the intervening community for months even after successful interventions. Some clients cannot express their appreciation for an intervention for months or years.

Consultation is also useful for those in authority. In the worse-case scenario the clinician assists the group to accept that ultimately the person is responsible for his or her recovery. Short of legal commitment, when applicable, the group must accept the person's freedom. Superiors and community members find acceptance difficult because they are accustomed to going the extra mile in helping others, often successfully. Education regarding the nature of addiction is helpful as is referral to Twelve-Step support groups such as Al-Anon.

Intervention and the Individual Clinician

The clinician who works alone, yet is competent in substance abuse treatment, can integrate the intervention process on an outpatient basis. However, this requires attention to the multidimensional nature of substance abuse, and accessing the required expertise at various points in the evaluation process. For example, mental health professionals will need to refer clients to medical specialists for a comprehensive evaluation.

The clinician who has limited experience with religious institutions may hesitate to initiate the essential institutional contacts for comprehensive treatment of addicted clients. The analogy of seeing the religious community as family is only partially accurate, as is viewing it as the employer. This also creates ethical questions. Who is the client? Is payment coming directly through the client, the client's insurance, or the client's employer? Expectations regarding information about the client need to be discussed at the outset of assessment to safeguard confidentiality and to permit appropriate communication of information to the referral source.

What may surprise the average clinician is how knowledgeable some communities are in coping with substance dependent members. Alcoholism recovery programs have long drawn avid interest from clergy who were among the first consultants to the founders of Alcoholics Anonymous, the only treatment resource for many "old-timer" religious professionals. Subsequent to their personal recovery many remained active in the substance abuse treatment field, even pioneering treatment approaches. Vernon Johnson, as noted above, refined the intervention process and established a training institute for alcoholism counselors that was a model for decades. Millions of Americans viewed and continue to view Father Joseph Martin's educational films on alcoholism. Others, including Father Martin, opened substance abuse treatment centers. Jesuit priest Father James Royce established the first graduate level program in alcohol studies in the United States at the University of Seattle. The benefit to the clinician, therefore, is that many religious institutions will have substance abuse specialists to consult with when determining patient disposition. These specialists are a most helpful resource for interpreting the culture of the religious institutions, yet have an excellent understanding of substance abuse dynamics. They also may provide suggestions for more intensive treatment programs, e.g., residential or day programs.

In summary, intervention, as proposed here, requires contact with the individual client, members of the relevant social groups, and an understanding of the religious community's organizational structure. Taken together, these systems have a powerful role for encouraging and motivating ambivalent or treatment-resistant clients to accept help.

TREATMENT AND THE CULTURE OF SHAME

Alcoholics Anonymous, in its intuitive wisdom, understood the social stigma attached to the label *alcoholic* and emphasized the importance of anonymity for creating the essential environment for members to address recovery issues without fear of social ostracism. The stigma associated with this label contributes to AA members reflecting deeply on the role that shame plays in the genesis and maintenance of active addiction. Some have described this in terms of doing battle with "the culture of shame." Readers familiar with psychoanalytic theory will recognize the traditional distinction here between violations of ego-ideal versus ego-conscience. The former, which results in shame, represents a failure to reach emotionally significant personal goals, often derived from the expectations of family or other social groups. The latter, which results in guilt, represents violation of rule-governed behavior. If shame plays such an important role in the dynamic of addictive behavior for the general member, how much more relevant is it for religious professionals?

The negative moral connotations that still exist in the majority culture toward alcoholism and alcoholics impact even further on this population. So many features of their normative self-definition run contrary to alcoholic behavior: personal control, living in accord with high standards, being a model of religious living, and seeing the self as one who exercises delay of gratification. The forces of denial in this population run deep. As the study described above indicates, many do not accept treatment until the disorder has progressed to the point of serious physical, neurological, and psychological damage. Because this study did not employ a comparison group of non-ministers, we do not know whether ministers receive treatment later than their lay counterparts, nor if this study generalizes to other than Roman Catholic clergy.

The social expectations for ministers in concert with the defense mechanism of denial conspire together to prevent the awareness of addiction in the minister's social network as well. Simply put, people do not readily suspect substance abuse as the explanation for unusual behavior in ministers.

Gender role expectations add further to the sources of denial, often preventing women ministers from identifying the source of their problem. Such expectations lead to ingenious methods to avoid detection.

Reverend Connie was associate pastor of a large Christian church in a sprawling suburban community. Her husband had challenged her about her drinking several months ago, and together they met with the pastor who was inclined to forgive and suggested she pray and overcome her problem with her family's help. She agreed to stop drinking, yet nightly during family time Connie's behavior showed evidence of intoxication. How this occurred was mysterious, especially in light of careful observation by her husband, daughter, and mother-in-law. They had removed alcohol from the home and observed her closely as she remained in the living room, only to notice drowsiness and slurring of speech. Only after Connie entered residential treatment did the family discover she had regularly filled a stash of her mother-in-law's insulin syringes with vodka and injected it into select oranges in the living room fruit bowl. She was careful to offer family members the untainted fruit even as she blissfully became inebriated before their watchful eyes.

For women ministers denial is sometimes so strong that even normally effective treatment methods do not crack the shell of denial as the following case attests.

Sister Maureen, a 52-year-old Roman Catholic sister, was referred to alcoholism treatment for bizarre interpersonal behavior in her community. Several times a week, in the evening, her normal, placid, and agreeable personality would change. She would express hostility to the other sisters in the form of biting sarcasm, critical statements, foul language, and an angry display of going to her room and slamming the door. Months of attempting to "understand" her problem led nowhere, as did outpatient counseling. The community became convinced that drinking was involved in her mood changes, an accusation she vehemently denied. Exasperated after finding multiple vodka bottles in the convent basement trash, her superior ordered her into treatment. After four months treatment in a specialized program for religious professionals, Sister Maureen held to her story that her drinking never entailed anything more than "a glass of wine on feast days." Exasperated themselves and divided over whether to accept her version of reality, the treatment staff released her. Only a year later were the facts evident when Sister Maureen's alcoholism had progressed to the point that other sisters witnessed her stumbling drunk.

As these examples indicate, colleagues and friends of women ministers are often at a loss because so much of the behavior that results in impairment is hidden. Substance abuse leads to ingenious methods for obtaining, hiding, and using alcohol and other drugs: putting empty bottles down laundry chutes, bicycling to liquor stores when car-restricted, and developing imaginary physical ailments to elicit prescriptions from physicians. Their addiction patterns often differ from men's, hence therapists need to attend to countertransference issues. Male patterns are not normative for women, whether in terms of the cycle of addiction or the cycle of recovery. In contrast to women who may go through several treatment programs denying the extent of their use, men often accept the extent of their drinking. They will, however, minimize its effects, or flaunt their personal autonomy. "*I'll* decide when I'm good and ready to stop." The severe stigma for women results in a more secretive pattern of use, a more focused emphasis on control, and greater psychological efforts to avoid the label of "alcoholic" or "addict."

The celibate culture, as we have emphasized, creates its own clinical challenges for successful intervention with substance abusing ministers. For married ministers the traditional intervention model is generally effective. The major complication is how social stigma prevents either (1) family members from openly discussing their difficulties and thereby getting the necessary social support to risk intervening; or (2) when they do speak out the social community invalidates their concerns, denying that the minister's drinking could be *that* bad. The following case illustrates this last point.

Reverend Tom, with a Congregational Church in New England, entered residential treatment in such a medically distraught state that the treatment team at first wondered if they could handle his physical needs. Tall, stately, and in his late fifties, he spoke with a carefully cultivated intellectual air. When detoxification began, however, his motor skills were so weakened that he could barely walk from tremulousness. Against normal procedures he was prescribed a small amount of Valium daily just to permit his walking erect. Although he maintained excellent conversational skills, neuropsychological testing revealed substantial cognitive impairment. The question for the treatment team was, how could someone who claimed he only drank "two glasses of vodka after dinner," display what looked like end-stage alcoholic deterioration? His spouse who was legally separated agreed to speak with treatment staff for one visit only, so long as it was not in his presence. She wanted to be clear that no reconciliation was possible. She described with considerable bitterness her attempts to motivate church council members to do something about her husband's drinking. Tom was an engaging fellow and his pleasant mood and verbal skills easily charmed his flock. Only after he drove his car through the parsonage living room wall trying to park it in the garage did the council vote to place him on medical leave. Hoping the spouse could shed light on Tom's physical condition, the team asked her about his "two glasses of vodka" each evening. She laughed sarcastically stating this was technically correct. Each evening Tom would fill two glass *blenders* with ice and vodka, drink them, and pass out drunk on the living room couch.

Integrating Spiritual Themes in Recovery

In assisting ministers with coming to terms with shame and guilt we may find it useful to distinguish religion from spirituality. Religion, a systematized body of beliefs and practices, may differ from personal spirituality. Personal spirituality may incorporate beliefs and practices from institutionalized religion, but may rely on practices that are not associated with their affiliated religious body. Spirituality can even exist totally independently from any religious institution, and comprises solely an attitude toward transcendence and what provides personal meaning.

In this manner, then, the Twelve-Step tradition is a program of spirituality with its foundation rooted in the acceptance of surrender to a Higher Power. This Higher Power may stand for the personal God of theistic religions or for any abstraction that motivates the individual to look beyond the self for meaning. Beyond the group's principles no formal creed exists, and members work out their spiritual journeys with group support and noninterference.

Some religious professionals need time adjusting to this concept. Heavily trained in and committed to the truth of a particular tradition, many religious professionals view the concept of spirituality without religion as at best disembodied. Others will view this as a form of idolatry to New Age beliefs or secular humanism. This mentality creates barriers to utilizing the group's power for recovery. Some will resist the program when they see theologically unlettered members expressing spiritual concepts they view as simplistic. They take refuge, therefore, in a defensive elitism. Others will intellectualize or attempt to proselytize using their denominational constructs. Members resist these attempts and so this interferes with the natural bonding that otherwise occurs in the group.

If there is some commitment to recovery, time usually overcomes these barriers. Most come to appreciate the beauty and diversity of spirituality inherent in the program. Many will begin to feel deficient when they view their own underdeveloped spirituality compared to members who have far fewer intellectual or educational gifts. Religious who bond with Twelve-Step programs often proselytize in reverse, enriching their own denominational practices with spiritual traditions from their program. Recovering alcoholic ministers report that, when greeting parishioners after the Sunday service, members comment discreetly, "Great sermon, Reverend. I'm a friend of Bill Wilson myself," which is code for membership in AA, the organization Wilson cofounded. The spiritual concepts delivered in their sermons give away their own identities as imbued in the tradition. For religious professionals who are prone to elitism obtaining a layperson sponsor with little formal education is an interesting antidote. This challenges the patient to get beyond the trappings and defenses of intellectualism to see the essence of spirituality. Such an intervention can have a Zen-like impact catapulting the patient into new perspectives.

Therapists need also attend to barriers from within the religious community toward Twelve-Step participation. We hope we are past the days when the nun had to wear a long black raincoat even on the sunniest days to disguise her rolled-up jeans underneath. She required this attire to sneak out of the convent to attend her AA meetings. When the elderly sisters in the convent would ask why she was wearing the raincoat she would reply, "Sister, the Lord wants us to be prepared." This mentality may exist in more subtle form today especially in groups that have strong community bonds. The underlying message is, "Why are you looking outside the community for your healing? If you simply invested yourself in our principles and practices, we would be sufficient for you." Such an attitude can cause self-alienation in recovering persons, torn between a necessary avenue for recovery and appearing disloyal to their traditions.

GAMBLING AND OVERSPENDING

Population studies reveal that about 1 to 3 people in 100 in the United States have a gambling problem (Ciarrocchi, 1992). This places its frequency in the same range as bipolar disorder, schizophrenia, or obsessive–compulsive disorder. Whether the same frequency exists within the population of religious professionals is difficult to determine since no study addresses this question. Certainly it does not appear in clinical samples with nearly the same frequency as substance abuse. The reasons for this are not totally clear. Social taboos against gambling in conservative religious groups may prevent the emergence of the disorder. Social taboo, however, does little to prevent alcohol-related problems. A more likely reason is the restricted availability of discretionary income. Ministers with families have such tight budgets to begin with that even a brief gambling fling would have immediate financial consequences. A rapid response to such losses from spouse or church boards most likely would result in further restricting monetary access. Priests' salaries, even taking into consideration room and board allowances, hover near the poverty line and most vowed religious make vows or promises of poverty. They either turn in their salaries and live on allowances, or keep a portion of their income paying a centralized allotment that functions as a tax.

We are discussing in this chapter problems associated both with gambling and overspending. In our experience the treatment regimen for each is similar. Both require stimulus control procedures around access to money as the first step. In the secular community males outnumber women pathological gamblers by about 2 to 1. Though one of us directed a large residential gambling treatment program that had male clergy patients, we do not personally know of women clergy or religious with a primary gambling disorder. We expect that rates of problem gambling for women religious professionals will increase as it does in secular society when women have greater economic resources. We are aware, however, of women clergy and religious with spending disorders. Male overspenders tend to resemble male gamblers' personality which we discuss in greater detail below. Female gamblers and overspenders resemble female substance abusers. The compulsive behavior often starts in one of two ways: (1) as a form of self-medication for negative affect; or (2) as a means of coping with a developmental crisis; e.g., widowhood, empty-nest syndrome, health problems, etc.

When gambling or overspending problems exist the clinician should assess if misappropriation of funds was the vehicle for obtaining money. The media periodically report scandals surrounding misuse or theft of church funds. Often gambling or compulsive spending is the cause because religious professionals have few other resources.

For the clinician who may be unfamiliar with the criteria for diagnosing pathological gambling the DSM criteria are straightforward. They parallel in many ways the criteria for substance dependence. They include a preoccupation with gambling, needing to increase the amount wagered to feel the desired excitement, agitation when unable to gamble, gambling to cope with negative affect, chasing losses, lying to others about the gambling, illegal behavior, needing others for financial bailouts, and causing relationship or occupational problems. The term *chasing* refers to throwing good money after bad in order to win back one's losses. Robert Custer (Custer & Milt, 1985), the psychiatrist who established the first gambling treatment program and who worked to include criteria for the condition in the DSM, described three stages in the disorder's evolution. Many gamblers experience a winning phase often punctuated by a "big win" equivalent to about six months' income. This whets the appetite for the possibilities of a gambling life-style. Eventually a losing phase sets in as the law of averages evens out the payoffs. This represents a crossroads. Most social gamblers learn to either quit gambling altogether or gamble within a restricted range of loss. Pathological gamblers move on to the desperation phase. Here chasing characterizes the gambling style.

We propose a crisis intervention model for treating the gambler or overspender at the outset. Abstinence control is the first task and requires the client to give up monetary control. For a religious professional an environmental resource is usually available. Whether a spouse, family member, or person designated by church authority controls expenditures, the client must no longer have sufficient funds available to feed the compulsion. Resolving the financial crisis is the next step. Clients need to be held accountable for their debts and significant others are counseled against bailing out the client. Money for treatment or legal defense is a usual exception, but otherwise clients develop payment plans for debts. Third, client and therapist must attend to any legal crisis by referral for legal advice. Therapists may need to consult with their own legal representatives regarding how to handle subpoenas or requests to testify. Fourth, therapists should be alert to risk assessment. As a group, about 20% of pathological gamblers report making a suicide attempt—a high rate for any single clinical entity. Finally, therapy must attend to the resultant marital or family crisis generated by gambling or overspending.

This population will naturally have a pastoral focus. Clients will have a more difficult time acknowledging an illness model for these conditions than they do for substance abuse. Their tendency is to view gambling as a moral failure. Even the most media-shy member of American culture has some sense that most people view alcoholism or drug addiction as an illness. Many, however, continue to view gambling and its resultant effects as sinful. The second major reflective therapeutic task is examining the function of the behavior for the person. For some it will serve as a distraction, a way to medicate themselves against intra- or interpersonal pain. Often we have seen gambling-spending function as relief from the pain of some sexual conflict. For others it will function as a way to develop self-esteem, to look and feel important. Many find it a heady mixture for their ego when casinos provide free meals and hotel rooms for high rollers. The attention gambling brings can be the last emotional refuge for the lonely, isolated, and alienated minister.

As with substance abuse treatment, Twelve-Step programs can be helpful. For gamblers there is Gamblers Anonymous (GA) and GamAnon, the program for families and friends of compulsive gamblers. For overspenders there is Debtors Anonymous (DA). We have conducted research that shows a considerable lag time in sense of family well-being between gamblers and their spouses. Gamblers in recovery through GA reported a sense of well-being comparable to population norms by the second year of recovery. A sense of family well-being, however, had not returned for gamblers' wives even after two or more years into recovery. For this reason we believe that conjoint therapy is a requirement for gambling treatment when gamblers are in a significant relationship.

7.

Sexual Problems

SEXUAL MISCONDUCT
AND COMPULSIVE SEXUAL BEHAVIOR

Clergy sexual misconduct in the last 10 years has sent shock waves through communities of believers. At the financial level after taking into consideration legal fees, payments to victims, treatment for perpetrators, etc., the costs are staggering. For the Catholic Church in the United States the total legal costs for pedophile cases alone is estimated eventually to total half a billion dollars (Berry, 1992).

Although less centralized, thus making statistical summary impossible, Protestant churches have also witnessed an explosion in the number of lawsuits against ministers for sexual misconduct. We can probably never know the full extent because churches and individual defendants settle many cases out of court to avoid either publicity or potentially more damaging jury trials. An added legal incentive to sue in the United States are antidiscrimination laws that permit legal redress when sexually "hostile environments" are created in a work setting. Sexual misconduct, then, may lead to legal sanctions in at least two ways: (1) when the misconduct occurs in a work setting, e.g., with a staff member; or (2) when it takes place with a congregant and thus represents a breach of trust. This latter form is similar to the dynamics of therapist sexual misconduct with a client (Gonsiorek, 1995; Rutter, 1989; Schoener, 1995; Sipe, 1990). To further complicate the legal situation some states have criminalized sexual contact between minister and congregant or have state task forces recommending such. Reading the signs of the times indicates that movement to criminalize such behavior is gaining favor with legislators and the public.

The cost to the perpetrators, obviously, is enormous: ruined careers, the shame of public scrutiny, and, in some instances, incarceration. Once convicted, states that enact so-called "Megan's laws" require convicted sexual felons to notify the local police of their residence. Originally intended to alert the community to child molestors the law casts its net broadly. A gay minister, for example, convicted of soliciting sex at an interstate restroom with an undercover police officer must identify himself to local police when changing residence.

The huge settlement costs speak of the psychological damage this behavior wreaks on its victims. Story after story emerges of victims grappling with broken marriages, failed relationships, histories of alcoholism, sexual orientation confusion, and myriad other symptoms associated with this trauma-inducing experience.

The toll on the faith community itself is incalculable. When personal faith is at the root of what gives life meaning and a revered spiritual figure behaves scandalously, the event forces a reexamination of one's very foundations. Those of us in the mental health field may have a tendency toward cynicism about institutions but we cannot lose sight of the deep personal hurt such behavior causes in followers. A member of the same denomination as Reverend Jimmy Swaggart began crying during his therapy session as he explored the sense of betrayal when the police discovered Swaggart in a motel with a known prostitute. The therapist felt awkward as he recalled how he had enjoyed the many jokes of a late-night television comedian told at Swaggart's expense. The therapist concentrated hard to provide the client with the accepting presence needed for him to work through a spiritual quest that had placed faith in someone undeserving of it.

Sexual misconduct demoralizes those who remain in professional ministry. Morale among dedicated clergy and religious professionals declines when their colleagues engage in sexual misconduct. Many describe feeling embarrassed when wearing a clerical collar after stories hit the media. They wonder if passersby imagine them to be child molesters. Others describe feeling hypervigilant when mingling with families or young people, wondering how every action or statement will be interpreted.

PROBLEM DEFINITION

Defining the entire range of sexual problems will help to develop individualized treatment goals for different clients. To develop a typology requires moving beyond the boundaries of standard DSM categories, since sexual misconduct includes a broader range of problem behavior. To review briefly, the DSM breaks sexual problems into two broad classes: paraphilia and sexual dysfunction; these are object-choice and sexual performance problems respectively. Sexual performance problems are not the focus of this chapter because our clinical experience indicates that traditional sex therapy models are effective. The exception is the occasional couple or individual whose inhibitory behavior prevents them from engaging in the relevant therapeutic exercises. Individuals from conservative religious backgrounds are more likely to have this characteristic.

The paraphilias are potentially a major category encompassing clergy sexual problems. Included here are problems such as pedophilia, voyeurism, frotteurism (anonymous sexual rubbing against or touching in crowded public places), and exhibitionism. Also included are disorders that fall in the 'Not-Otherwise-Specified' (NOS) category. These include ephebophilia (sexual contact with pubertal minors), and telephone scatologia (making obscene phone calls or compulsive use of commercial sexual phone services). Additionally clinicians might see other clinical types among clergy and religious such as persons who are fixated on pornography, prostitution, or even masturbation.

Sexual problems, however, encompass a broader range of sexual behavior than DSM disorders. Sexual misconduct for clergy and vowed religious includes behavior that is ultimately social misconduct and as such, may or may not fall within the boundaries of mental disorders. One pattern of sexual misconduct presents as a fixated, repetitive, compulsive variety that the client experiences as a preoccupation whether in fantasy or acted out. The chosen behavior varies among types, e.g., pornography, soliciting prostitutes, or frequenting massage parlors. But in any event the word *addicted* easily comes to mind in describing the behavior. This behavior may result in sexual misconduct if it enters the public dimension, especially if it violates an ethical or professional norm. Having sex with one's counselee is sexual misconduct; compulsive use of pornographic material is not, if the person procures and uses the material privately. However, even here private compulsive use of sexual materials and misconduct may become intertwined. In the United States the First Amendment no longer protects child pornography so that involvement in its use is illegal. Recently federal authorities arrested several men in a child pornography "sting" operation. One of those arrested was a priest who taught moral theology in a seminary.

A second pattern of sexual misconduct presents as an isolated example of inappropriate sexual behavior, one that does not indicate a repetitive pattern. In her doctoral dissertation, pastoral counselor Geradine Taylor (1996) studied personality profiles of 80 Roman Catholic priests in treatment for sexual misconduct. For half, the misconduct represented compulsive, repetitive patterns; for the other half it represented infrequent behavior or was limited to few episodes. Using the MMPI, the Millon Clinical Multiaxial Inventory, and the NEO-PI (a test of normal personality based on the so-called Big Five factor model; Piedmont, 1998), she was able to distinguish reliably between the two groups. The compulsive group had significantly higher symptoms of negative affect (anxiety, depression, hostility, impulsivity, vulnerability, self-consciousness) and were less conscientious than the episodic group. The episodic group appeared relatively healthy from a symptom standpoint as measured by these tests. However, on the personality disorder measure both groups had high scores and high rates of dependent personality disorder. Taylor's study suggests that compulsive sexual misconduct represents a variant of severe, chronic psychological distress characterized by intense emotional pain with few internal controls. A second pattern results from overly dependent clergy who reach out initially to help but who cross boundaries when the encounter triggers their own personal emotional needs.

To return to the diagnostic question some impulsive sexual behavior might not meet DSM criteria for mental disorders. Mere rule-breaking does not qualify as a disorder according to DSM definitions. The *consequences*, for example, of committing adultery or violating celibacy may *lead* to symptoms of psychological distress which then constitute a disorder. But the acts themselves are not technically a disorder. Repetitive sexual misconduct, however, probably falls under the not otherwise specified (NOS) category (i.e., when a mental disorder is of a certain class but specific criteria are lacking. For example, passive–aggressive personality disorder is personality disorder, NOS). Taylor's research raises the question as to whether substance use disorders might provide an analogy for sexually exploitative behavior. Perhaps compulsive exploitation is to episodic exploitation what substance dependence is to substance abuse. A distinguishable nosology between types of exploitative behavior will also have important treatment implications. One would expect a lesser impairment level and greater treatment response from the episodic group based on the degree of psychopathology alone.

CULTURAL ASPECTS OF SEXUAL PROBLEMS

In a religious professional population moral standards may rule out behaviors that the majority culture views as acceptable. Attitudes will vary within and among religious groups toward such experiences as masturbation, sexually oriented visual materials, or intentionally creating in the mind a sexual mental fantasy. When this occurs therapists should attend to countertransference issues. One tendency is to influence the client toward behaviors acceptable to the therapist. In the case described in chapter 6, a therapist refused to work with a seminarian who wanted help in reducing the frequency of masturbation. Informed consent requires that clients collaborate in the selection and implementation of treatment goals. Obtaining this consent involves discussing not only the treatment goal but also the methods for attaining the goal. Client ethical conflicts may arise in either case.

A cultural barrier to clinical resolution of sexual problems is the social constraints placed on developing alternative coping skills.

> Pastor Frank, a 33-year-old associate pastor of a large fundamentalist Protestant church, newly recovering from alcoholism, reveals that when drinking he became overly friendly with teenage boys. Although he has not acted on these sexual impulses with them, he realizes that his conversation is inappropriate. He fears that, if drunk enough, he might go farther sexually. His history suggests a homosexual orientation, although he has never had relational sexual experiences, nor a reciprocal romantic relationship. He firmly believes that a homosexual lifestyle, even between consenting adults, is sinful. He even believes the Bible condemns the homosexual status in people, so this further complicates therapeutic guidance toward self-discovery. He is willing to accept the possibility that he is homosexual but he is firm in his need to remain celibate. He rules out marriage, for the moment, as he evaluates his sexual orientation. He appreciates now that he used alcohol to suppress forbidden sexual thoughts.

If this case involved someone not committed to celibacy, the therapist would, no doubt, recommend that the client establish healthy peer relationships. More than likely establishing intimacy would be the treatment goal.

But since this case involves a person who sees celibacy as the only option, the therapist must assess Frank's interests. As indicated in the chapter on celibacy, several answers are possible. He might identify the problem as remaining celibate and want to seek adult intimacy as soon as possible, without intending a decision about leaving ministry. A second position could be remaining sexually abstinent, while establishing a network of gay friends who could provide support and understanding. A third position views homosexuality as a self-definition and one that is sinful. In this case he might desire to recover from his alcohol problems with no connection to the gay world or life-style.

What might be appropriate for nonclergy might, for clergy, carry with it untoward risks for social ostracism or even cost them their jobs. Treatment plans, therefore, have to take this cultural context into consideration lest greater harm befall the client. The degree of inhibition may strike the therapist as extreme yet is quite real as this ironic case illustrates.

George was a 24-year-old seminarian preoccupied with male adolescent sexual imagery. He thought he might experience relief if he could shift his sexual fantasies from adolescents to adults. The therapist assessed that George found male fantasies attractive for younger persons but preferred females sexually as adults. The therapist suggested that masturbating to fantasies of adult women might decrease his preoccupation with teenage boys, and that this might help reorient his sexual interests, if not altogether eliminate his attachment to minors. The problem of obtaining the requisite visual stimuli remained a thorny one for George. He related his utter embarrassment about purchasing a men's magazine from a convenience store. In exploring what the client feared, he recounted a fantasy of the store clerk calling attention to the purchase in some way in front of other customers thus humiliating the client. No amount of reassurance from the therapist that he had seen hundreds of customers purchase such material in stores without once observing such a scene could allay his fear. The therapist, therefore, arranged to see George at his final session and together they walked around the corner to a convenience store. Taking the client's money he walked up to the clerk and asked for the magazine. The client stood off to the side as a line of about half-a-dozen customers grew. In this case the adult magazine racks were behind another counter about 10 feet away. The clerk walked over to the rack, took out one copy of each magazine, held them high in the air, and shouted in a voice that could be heard around the block, "Which one do you want? I bet it's the one with Bo Derek."

The risk-taking for developing alternative skills to sexual problems often involves greater potential negative consequences than purchasing an adult magazine.

DYNAMICS OF SEXUAL MISCONDUCT

The majority of clinical experience in treating sexual misconduct arises from treating sexual offenders referred through the legal system. Generally high rates of antisocial personality disorder characterizes this group, or, at a minimum, antisocial personality traits. Generalizing from this population to the religious professional, even in the case of sexual misconduct, misses the unique dynamics at play for clergy offenders.

To understand this dynamic, recourse to the classic sociodemographic profile of the male pedophile is instructive. Contrary to popular imagination pedophiles are not "dirty old men" who, as a group, advocate man–child sexual politics. The average offender is a younger or middle-aged man whose political views are socially and morally conservative. When we exclude the serial killers, or "lust-murders" in John Money's terminology, the pedophile offender often mirrors the stereotypical "pillar of the community." They are usually religious individuals whose opinions are traditional and even conservative. When examining the person's life-style the word *hypocrisy* easily comes to mind. This was the thrust of much public commentary when a politically and religiously conservative Maryland congressman was convicted on charges of soliciting sex with a teenage boy. The experienced clinician, however, sees another force at work. Operating here is the classic dynamic of psychological splitting, the person who cannot integrate powerful sexual urges and attraction with equally powerful forces that view sexual impulses as evil. As tension builds, acting out followed by intense self-recrimination resolves the split temporarily. Acting out both fulfills the sexual urge and the need to inflict punishment for one's drives. Learning theory adds to this dynamic by assuring the repetition of this pattern via the powerful reinforcing biological rewards from sexual experience.

Familiarity with this dynamic within human behavior implies that we have a ready interpretation for clergy sexual misconduct and this model is heuristic for treatment planning. Although the behavior may shock or outrage us, for clinicians the dynamics are clear. Further, the dynamics suggest that we should not express surprise that religious communities would have more than their fair share of sexual offenders. Without confusing correlation with causation we would expect that persons with this psychosocial profile naturally gravitate toward social groups that share their worldview. All things being equal, religious institutions are generally communities of conservation and tradition.

THERAPEUTIC STRATEGIES

Because a nonjudgmental environment is crucial to treating these conditions, we emphasize this therapeutic dimension. Steeped in our sense of the dignity of the person we may not attend to our client's expectations or actual experience.

In a group therapy session with alcoholic clergy inpatients a priest told how he transferred on three different buses to attend individual therapy with the only Catholic psychiatrist he could find willing to treat him [in the 1960s]. The client wanted to work on his emerging awareness of a homosexual orientation and its implications. He was aware that when he drank, sexual fantasies about teenage boys emerged. Every group participant, therapists as well as patients, became tearful when he told his therapist's response, "Reverend, I will be able to treat you, but you will need to turn your chair away from me so that I only see your back. Otherwise I'm afraid my negative feelings toward all that you've said will interfere with treatment." Members cried as they reflected on this client's passive acceptance of two years of therapy under these circumstances.

Before we address specific sexual problems in this population we will outline the various strategies for intervening. Empirically validated therapies for sexual misconduct are sparse, so this section represents greater eclecticism than previous chapters.

Functional Assessment

A functional, analytic approach to assessment is useful in two ways. First, through its matter-of-fact emphasis on the behavioral components of the sexual problem, it simultaneously gathers data efficiently and creates an objective, nonjudgmental atmosphere. As clients respond to the "who, what, when, where, why, how, how often, etc.," laundry list of assessment questions, they learn to defocus from the emotive aspects that cloud self-acceptance. Second, behavioral analysis is most fruitful in teaching clients the concept of a behavioral "chain," as in the chain of events related to acting out. Clients tend to view their behavior as impulsive, mysterious, or outside their control, as the result of overwhelming environmental forces or characterological defects. A minute emphasis on the sequence of events leading to as many episodes as the client can recall will establish the correlative links to acting out.

Crucial to this task of behavioral analysis is self-monitoring of sexual urges. As emphasized in our discussion of other problems, self-monitoring provides concurrent validation of any hypotheses client and therapist develop about predicting high-risk situations. As assessment proceeds a variety of behavioral strategies is available. We will describe some of these techniques in this section but a caution is in order. Many of these strategies evolved out of single-case experimental studies or in studies involving incarcerated offenders. We need to be cautious about the degree of generalizability from the criminal justice system to religious professionals. We will note how we have tailored these strategies for use with religious professionals.

Stimulus Control Strategies

Arranging the external environment is one way to reduce the probability of an identified sexual behavior. In the area of dieting one way to cut down on eating chocolate is to not bring it into the house. Otherwise, having boxes of fudge in the refrigerator creates an unnecessary high-risk condition for binge eating. Psychologist Daniel Wegner (1989) coined the term *remote control* for this strategy. Using remote control means people do not laboriously struggle with the multiple decisions that bombard and wear them down when environments continually beckon them.

Remote control solutions emerge *after* a detailed assessment and are always individualistic. If a chain analysis indicates that cruising sexual behavior is always linked to purchasing the city paper that lists sex-for-pay phone numbers, then remote control involves strategies to prevent purchasing the paper. The client may need to drive intentionally three blocks out of his way home from work to avoid passing the newsstand. Remote control implies that in the chain sequence personal control decreases the closer a person approaches the final link. In the early stages of recovery it is unrealistic to expect restraint at the penultimate link but control is possible farther back in the chain.

The case of avoiding the newsstand represents direct circumvention of the physical location. In other situations, however, people cannot totally avoid places so remote control might involve strategies directed at influencing *time*, thereby interjecting a delay mechanism into the chain.

> Pat, a Lutheran seminarian who masturbated compulsively, indicated that social encounters were capable of distracting him from this behavior. He lived in a college dorm so finding others around day or night was seldom a problem. With the assistance of his therapist he created a delay link in the chain by agreeing to masturbate only after he had visited someone else in the dorm for a minimum of 20 minutes. This significantly reduced the frequency of masturbation and had the added benefit of decreasing his social isolation. He felt better about himself viewing himself as less self-centered.

Other remote control strategies include using naturally occurring environmental constraints to make oneself accountable.

> Zachary, an Assembly of God pastor, was prone to visit massage parlors when traveling to another state to visit his father in a nursing home. He changed this by calling his father just as he was leaving the house to give an arrival time. He always gave a time that coincided almost to the minute with the actual travel time. Knowing that his father tended to worry about his safety

should he arrive late motivated him to bypass the massage parlor.

Negative Strategies

Self-applied punishment may also deter the problem sexual behavior. One method is overt, one covert. An uncomplicated *covert* form is for the client to list all the negative outcomes related to the behavior. The following represents a step-by-step format.

1. Through discussion or guided imagery the client recalls the aftermath of a recent acting-out episode, one that had particularly negative consequences or which represented a high risk for such.
2. The client records in writing or on audiotape the precise details of the post-episode scenario. In particular the client attends to the negative feelings of shame and guilt. Appropriate to this description are feelings about failing to restrain his behavior, the actual or potential consequences of discovery, its effect on commitments, relationships, and ministry.
3. The client records the physical, psychological, spiritual, and interpersonal costs of this behavior.
4. When an urge to act out reaches an agreed-upon level of intensity, the client takes out this record and reviews it slowly and thoughtfully.
5. Should he relapse, he reviews the original description and amends further negative feelings or experiences to make the scene more vivid for future prevention.

Overt strategies (punishment or response cost in behavior therapy terms) involve applying material negative consequences after the client acts out to decrease repeating the behavior. Client and therapist might work out an arrangement to make a donation to a personally repugnant group or organization. A liberal person could donate an agreed-upon sum to the Christian Coalition, a conservative to the American Civil Liberties Union.

Substituting Adaptive Behavior

Life-style imbalance increases probability for acting out across a wide range of behavior problems. Improving the balance between "shoulds" and "wants" can help relieve the urgency of impulses to act out inappropriately. Many of the suggestions in chapter 1 for reducing stress are relevant here as well. Furthermore, a chain analysis often finds that negative reactions to interpersonal conflict precede acting out. Learning alternative interpersonal coping skills such as anger control or assertiveness training may avoid the emotional precursors to the problem behavior.

Sexual Fantasy Therapies

In a limited number of cases sexual fantasy therapies may have a place. When the sexual fantasies are troublesome in themselves or are associated with acting inappropriately, change strategies directed toward the fantasies themselves are appropriate. One set of change strategies involves the client privately using the problem sexual fantasy to initiate sexual arousal, and then switching to a more appropriate image as climax approaches. Case reports found that by repeating these trials some persons with deviant sexual fantasies were able to experience arousal more readily to appropriate sexual situations.

Two caveats are in order for this technique. In controlled studies the effects of this procedure are weak even though individual case reports are positive. The second is that autoerotic practices are inherently unethical in some religious traditions. These traditions (e.g., Roman Catholicism) hold that to masturbate even for the purpose of decreasing pedophile behavior is using an evil means to attain a good end and therefore immoral.

A second strategy described in the behavior therapy literature with sex offenders is *satiation therapy*. This procedure involves masturbating in private at great length to the deviant sexual imagery *after* reaching orgasm (e.g., for 60 to 90 minutes). As the name implies, satiation works as an aversive conditioning procedure to reduce the impulse to achieve sexual satisfaction using the preferred but deviant fantasies. Research studies are more promising for this technique, but, again, ethical restraints may prevail with some clients.

Education

Education also has its place in the therapeutic armamentarium. Although every clinician is aware of the limits of simply imparting information, the lack of basic sexual information in this population may startle even a seasoned therapist. The clinician may encounter naiveté even of basic biological facts of sexual reproduction or misinformation regarding protection from disease. Taking a detailed sexual history ensures not missing such deficiencies. Some in this population will not have experienced an orgasm. Others will ruminate about sexual matters even in the absence of experience.

> Albert was a Methodist minister who had devoted his life to reaching the poor in geographically inaccessible rural areas. He developed alcoholism and entered residential treatment. Following detoxification he told his counselors about his obsession that he was homosexual. He denied any interpersonal sexual contact of any sort. His sexual history revealed he could not recall ever having an orgasm, not even through a wet dream. Despite the absence of experience he was preoccupied that somehow or another homosexuality was his "condition." His low sexual drive did not prevent feeling constant guilt about his potential sexual orientation. Psychiatric evaluation discounted the belief as a delusion.

In many cases information combined with empathic understanding will reassure the client. For example, a male clergyman revealed intense guilt on the few occasions per month that he masturbated. Clinical assessment revealed that the guilt was most intense immediately after orgasm and he was interpreting the natural postorgasmic lull as God's shaming punishment. He achieved enormous relief when the clinician reattributed the postorgasmic lull to natural physiological letdown.

Self-Help Groups

A variety of self-help groups, some modeled on Twelve-Step programs, are available in urban areas to provide adjunctive therapeutic support. Names vary according to region and include Sexaholics Anonymous or Sex and Love Addicts Anonymous. Some of these groups view compulsive sexual behavior as an addiction and receive their inspiration from popular books such as Patrick Carnes' *Don't Call It Love* (1991). Within the variety of compulsive sexual behavior and "love addiction" members have latitude to develop a personal plan of recovery. Analogous to Overeaters' Anonymous, total abstinence is not required but recovery plans revolve around members' so-called "bottom line," a range of sexual behaviors from which they choose to abstain. Groups have many of the traditional supports to Twelve-Step groups such as anonymity, sharing their stories, choosing a sponsor, etc. Clergy seem to bond well to these groups and benefit from the emphasis on spirituality which is similar to AA groups.

Therapists need to attend to potential conflict between self-help models and psychological strategies. As with AA the conflict is more imagined than real, involving many points of convergence between the two approaches. One conflict is the emphasis on fantasy restraint, which appears to contradict the mindfulness/acceptance strategy discussed below. Clients may view mindfulness as one step in acquiring fantasy restraint. A second problem is common to Twelve-Step programs, namely the tendency to view clergy-participants as "experts" in the area of spirituality. This will distract clergy-members from paying attention to their own spiritual deficits in the guise of helping others.

Mindfulness-Acceptance

A promising approach involves a set of procedures that go by a variety of terms such as *mindfulness* (Kabat-Zinn, 1990; Langer, 1989; Linehan, 1993), *sensory awareness* (Perls, Hefferline, & Goodman, 1951), *acceptance* (Hayes, 1994; LoPiccolo, 1994;

Marlatt, 1994). The essence of this strategy is dealing with intense sexual fantasies by accepting them rather than trying to suppress them. Supported by studies that demonstrate thought suppression actually increases the production of undesirable images, acceptance therapy promotes shifting perspective around the obsessional idea to defuse its psychological power. Clinical research, to date, has focused this strategy on four areas: (1) training persons with borderline personality disorders to control impulsive behaviors such as parasuicidal urges (Linehan, 1993); (2) enriching the living situations of the elderly (Langer, 1989); (3) reducing cravings in alcoholics and drug abusers (Marlatt, 1994); and (4) promoting health-enhancing behaviors via stress reduction (Kabat-Zinn, 1990). Clinicians have also described its use with ego-dystonic sexual obsessions for person with OCD (Ciarrocchi, 1995a), and for ego-syntonic sexual obsessions in the treatment of paraphilia (LoPiccolo, 1994).

Clergy and vowed religious are particularly susceptible to the negative impact of thought suppression. Schooled in willful self-control strategies that emphasize taking charge over one's "lower" instincts they inadvertently increase both the salience and frequency of the forbidden thoughts. Wegner's (1989) research on the "white-bear" phenomenon demonstrates that thoughts will *increase* in frequency following attempts to suppress them. People cannot *not* think of white bears once the idea of suppressing the image is suggested to them. This helps explain the paradox described earlier in the association between religious and political conservatism and pedophilia. The very horror of the fantasy leads to intense efforts to suppress the thoughts which has the white-bear effect of increasing them.

Mindfulness-acceptance is the exact opposite of thought suppression. Marlatt captures the core of acceptance therapy with his image of "urge surfing." He likens obsessional thoughts, urges, or images to a wave upon the mind's ocean. They rise and fall with greater or lesser intensity; but they always move on. Coping with these thought waves is similar to skillful surfing. Rather than throwing one's body against the breakers and getting knocked down, the person goes with the flow and uses the wave's power to glide across the water. Surfing one's thoughts involves "observing, describing, and not judging" the images as they rise and fall across the mind. Linehan describes this strategy well in her excellent manual for the treatment of borderline personality disorder which also includes client handouts.

This strategy is advantageous for our population whether the sexual images are ego dystonic (the scrupulous) or ego syntonic (paraphilias). For some religious professionals, as we noted in the section on treating OCD, sexual images and fantasies are undesirable and intrusive. For them the need to perform the compulsion functions as an overvalued idea, i.e., it feels almost rational within their own logical system. To suggest exposure and response prevention techniques can generate resistance because it feels sinful to them to instigate sexual imagery intentionally. Mindfulness is usually acceptable because they understand it as a strategy to reduce the sexual obsession rather than to promote immoral thoughts.

Mindfulness strategies may also help the therapeutic process by minimizing countertransference issues. Some therapists are mystified when religious clients maintain that it is immoral to have a sexual feeling or thought toward someone unless you are married to them. The therapist's impulse is to engage the client in a dialogue around the value or effect of such a belief. Such a dialogue will often backfire. Therapists do not always have the theological background to understand the cultural context of such beliefs. Recall years ago the wave of mirth from the media when President Jimmy Carter admitted in an interview with *Playboy* magazine to the sin of "lust in the heart." Many mocked his acceptance of what is a biblically based moral maxim shared by many Christians. Second, as motivational interviewing theory suggests, attempts to persuade clients of alternative views simply trigger reactance and force them to elaborate further arguments for their position. With mindfulness the therapist accepts clients where they are and allows them to experience the ebb and flow of *all* images, desirable and undesirable alike.

At the other end of the continuum the paraphilias represent images that are ego syntonic similar to how an alcoholic experiences drinking urges or a smoker the desire for cigarettes. For them mindfulness or urge surfing is a strategy that helps break the impulsive connection between thought and behavior. They learn that, although they cannot control their thoughts any more than they can suppress waves on the ocean, they can resist acting out as the solution for obtaining relief from the urges. Instead they focus on the images from the perspective of an "observing mind" or that of a "reporter" who observes and describes the image in a detached, neutral manner. The person continues this description until the intensity of the impulse to act out diminishes to a manageable level. In this technique the person combines a descriptive narration while self-monitoring the intensity to act out as the following scenario suggests.

> Reverend Alex, a pastor in a United Church of Christ congregation, finds one aspect of his preconversion youth maddeningly repetitive. Although he feels committed to his marriage and family, he battles continuously with urges to have sex with prostitutes. Every two or three months he gives in to the impulses, but he battles them several times a week.

The numbers in brackets represent, on a scale of 1 to 10, the intensity of urges to act out. The scenario revolves around Reverend Alex's impulse to have sex with a prostitute. He is driving home from a frustrating regional meeting and will pass the interstate exit near a massage parlor he has visited in the past.

> I just saw the billboard for the McDonald's sign announcing the exit to the massage parlor. I always stop at that McDonald's after I go there. I am feeling so frustrated and I remember that drop-dead beauty I met there the last time, more beautiful than a fashion model [10]. God, I don't think I can stand it. Wait, the strategy is I'm supposed to think about this as if I'm a reporter, just observing and describing, but not judging. How can I not judge when it feels so deliciously forbidden? OK, back to the strategy. I'm supposed to be aware and monitor myself *reacting* here and now. Well I'm certainly aware that I am reacting sexually, in fact I'm highly aroused. This is about as aroused as I get [10]. I feel an intense urge to want to visit the parlor, to make

contact with someone, and have that person smile sweetly at me and act like they care about me. This makes me feel important, that I *am* somebody, that someone will comfort me. My breathing is a little calmer now [9]. I'm thinking of how we negotiate the fee for services. A little exciting because I know what's next but also degrading. I know I'm only important as a cash commodity but they certainly put on a good act [8]. I'm imagining that we're having sex, it seems like heaven, so incredibly intense, and now it's over. I'm feeling physically satisfied in some way but I also notice I'm alone, by myself, no cuddling, no warmth, no tenderness [7]. I'm running late now; I'm thinking of how to cover the money I spent [7]. I still have the urge to have sex; it feels attractive, but I'm aware that there are some real costs [6]. I'm aware that in the time I've spent just observing and describing, my sexual interest has decreased [5]. This means it comes and goes, it doesn't stay at a crazy-making level constantly. In fact, when that jerk in the Camaro swerved in front of me to make that last exit, I forgot completely about it [3].

This scene may represent only the first wave of the acceptance strategy for this event. Reverend Alex may need to keep at this scenario as he continues to drive down the turnpike until he feels able to drive by the exit. This "urge surfing" process teaches the client that sexual urges may appear to hit like a crescendo but in reality have an ebb and flow that permits self-direction. Mindfulness is a skill that clients can acquire for purposes other than "temptation." We have highlighted its usefulness for stress reduction and we think it is essential that clients who wish to use it for sexual coping practice the technique in nonsexual situations. The behavioral concept of over-learning will ensure that the automatic nature of mindfulness honed from multiple scenarios will more readily generalize to the crucial domain of sexual compulsivity. For that reason we suggest practicing mindfulness throughout the day in situations both routine and tension-filled. This attention to awareness for even repetitive "mindless" activities fits in with many Eastern and Western forms of spirituality and mysticism, and these clients usually spontaneously make that connection in the course of practice. This may further motivate them to see the value in the strategy thereby enhancing its effectiveness.

SPECIFIC BEHAVIOR PROBLEMS

Overall Strategy

At this point discussion of an overall strategy for the clinician is necessary. As is evident, the wide range of problems discussed here involves varying degrees of therapist experience and training. Treating some ministers requires considerable background not available to the average clinician while others require a mixture of standard competency, information, and common sense. To simplify the decision process let us consider the entire range of clinical intervention as encompassing assessment, short-term treatment, and long-term follow-up.

The assumption here is that the first stage involves broad range assessment to put the problem sexual behavior in its larger context. Short-term treatment focuses on reducing or eliminating the target behavior. Follow-up intervention looks to maintain initial gains and alter more embedded psychological features that could potentially trigger relapse. Clinicians can utilize this model to determine where on the continuum they should offer their services. This decision will vary according to the specific problem and the individual clinician. Minimum involvement is straight referral without further contact. A number of specialty programs exist for the evaluation of sexual problems in the general public or religious professionals. Most offer the option of short-term and long-term treatment when client resources permit. These programs provide clinician and client with options to work together or apart for various phases of treatment. In a specific case clinicians may want to handle one phase of treatment but not another. This is very similar to what takes place with addiction counseling, where the interest or ability for primary substance abuse treatment varies among therapists.

Pedophilia and Ephebophilia

As an active problem the best advice for pedophilia is to refer the person to a specialty program. Referral meets the client needs in two major ways. First, criminal law invariably requires reporting the perpetrator and specialty programs monitor comprehensive systems including required reporting of abuse and appropriate legal referral for the client. Second, disorders involving consequences of such magnitude require full-range medical, neuropsychological, and psychosocial assessment by specialists trained in ferreting out information from all possible sources.

As noted above the clinical and legal definitions of pedophilia are distinct. The DSM diagnosis involves repetitive fantasies or behavior directed toward *pre*pubescent minors, while the legal definition involves sexual touching of *any* amount with *any* minor, prepubescent or not. This further reinforces the necessity of specialized assessment. Since all acts of sexual touching of a minor are illegal, but not all acts constitute a mental disorder (e.g., rape is strictly a criminal act), the clinician stands on safer grounds if the diagnosis emanates from a team of specialists rather than an individual therapist.

Take, for example, the alcoholic religious professional who sexually touched a youngster only occasionally in the past and always under the influence of alcohol. Too much is at stake for client, clinician, and society to be certain that recovery from alcoholism means the client is not at risk to repeat the offense. If the client indeed represents a minimal risk, the clinician can proceed prudently when a specialized team has reached that conclusion. The same guidelines are recommended when the sexual contact is between a religion professional and a pubescent minor (adolescent). This is not DSM pedophilia and technically falls under Sexual Disorder, Not Otherwise Specified. Treatment specialists coined the term "ephebophilia" to describe this disorder. Although the characteristics of the perpetrators are rather different from those of pedophiles, the same practical referral strategy makes sense due to the legal and social implications.

Rehabilitation of pedophiles, in the strict diagnostic sense, has many obstacles. As a group they share to a greater degree the qualities described above regarding the dynamics of compulsive sexual behavior in religious persons. As Masters and Johnson noted over 20 years ago, those with rigid religious backgrounds are recalcitrant to changing their sexual behavior. The other quality that tends to puzzle clinicians is a form of distortion that is quasi-delusional. Some pedophiles experience the adult analogue of falling in love with their victims. When this occurs they describe their "relationship" with the victim in language usually associated with romantic love. The victim "cares" for him and vice versa. They "share" their innermost thoughts with each other, and "confide" in each other. Victims "wound" the adult through "neglect." Nabakov's novel, *Lolita*, with its ironic observations on this motif reaches comic proportions, a quality not mirrored in the clinical reality. When the clinician first encounters this phenomenon a disorienting effect is possible. He or she finds periodic "reality checks" necessary as a reminder that the client is projecting onto an 8-year-old the emotional capacity of a 25-year-old.

Comprehensive rehabilitation usually includes individual and group therapy as well as self-help group participation. Programs will require or recommend antiandrogen medication for men to provide a respite from impulsive sexual acts. Freed from the daily onslaught of compulsion the client can develop psychosocial skills to handle sexuality appropriately.

Ephebophilia shares some characteristics of pedophilia but clinical experience suggests better general rates of recovery. Alcoholism is often comorbid with this condition. A common subset for this dual diagnosis in male clergy or religious is an unintegrated homosexual orientation. In these cases the therapeutic tasks are straightforward: alcoholism recovery, resolution of the sexual orientation conflict, and restraint of inappropriate sexual behavior. The technical difficulty is that all tasks must occur concomitantly requiring considerable skill in managing each aspect of treatment. Residential treatment assists this enterprise because it provides an environmental safety net to explore all these issues and minimizes acting out should the client feel overwhelmed.

When unintegrated homosexual orientation stands alone with ephebophilia the clinical issues are identical to those described in chapter 8 under the culture of sexuality for persons who choose celibacy. Otherwise the minister's decision to develop appropriate adult sexual partners guides the therapeutic task. We address the treatment issues for this problem in the next section. The major assessment task with ephebophilia is determining whether it is developmentally fixated, as is often the case, or situation-dependent. When not fixated developmentally the person with ephebophile tendencies can shift his focus to cultivate intimacy with appropriate peers.

Considerable controversy swirls around the topic of rehabilitation for pedophilia, ephebophilia, or other forms of sexual exploitation and whether one can ever justify a return to ministry. Since treatment takes place in a social–legal context, these factors have changed the climate for treatment and follow-up. The first factor, of course, is that some forms of exploitation are illegal (e.g., pedophiliac behavior) and result in criminal prosecution. However, many cases clinicians deal with do not fall in this category. These include cases in which the charges are already adjudicated or those where lack of evidence or statutes of limitation prevent prosecution. Even where no criminal sanctions are possible civil suits are often permissible so that liability for client, religious institution, and possibly clinician may remain.

A second factor at work is a considerable movement to hold *all* helping professionals strictly accountable for sexual misconduct in the conduct of their occupation. Every reader is aware how this concern translates into each profession scrutinizing its own ethical codes, adopting new guidelines, and increasing sanctions against sexual exploitation by its members. Jurisdictions either have or are considering laws that criminalize treatment exploitation including that perpetrated by clergy. Even if the clinician believes that the probability of future exploitation is inconsequential, the minister's religious institution may judge the risks to the community's personal and material well-being unacceptable. In these situations the therapeutic task shifts from rehabilitation with the goal of reentry into ministry to transition into an alternative occupation (cf. chapter 9 on transitions).

Furthermore, the particular structure of authority in the client's social group will influence the therapeutic task. Institutions with decentralized authority structures can take swift action to discharge the offender from their ranks. Others in highly centralized institutions (e.g., Roman Catholicism) have elaborate legal systems with procedures that ensure individual rights much the way a constitution ensures citizen rights. If a sister or brother, for example, cooperates with treatment, ordinarily the religious community cannot discharge him or her and may even have certain obligations of support. For self and community protection the organization will refuse the person a religious assignment and require him to obtain secular employment. But ecclesiastical law may permit him to remain within the organization even without an active ministry.

Researchers and clinicians are debating the entire issue of rehabilitation from sexual misconduct and what criteria to follow, if any, for returning offenders to their previous work. As the debate currently exists some take the position that the safer course is for no return to the previous occupation. The argument is based on the lack of valid measures to predict recidivism. This position applied to clergy would advocate no return to active ministry. Others point to high rates of recovery for many treated in specialty programs with few reports of recidivism. They describe subsets of clinical types that both on a priori grounds and treatment experience justify reasonable cause for returning to ministry. These observations, although certainly sincere, are not confirmed by independent outcome studies as yet. The clinician, therefore, needs to attend to the entire context and consult with knowledgeable individuals in the psychological, legal, and religious communities before establishing goals related to ministry.

TREATMENT ISSUES FOR GAY AND LESBIAN MINISTERS

Recently a diocese in the Episcopal Church in the United States attempted to excommunicate a bishop who ordained to the priesthood a homosexual man who acknowledged publicly living in a sexually active relationship with a committed partner. The charge of heresy for this act on the bishop's part was not upheld. The Roman Catholic Church, which requires celibacy for the majority of its clergy and all vowed religious, describes homosexual behavior in its official documents as "disordered."

Catholic intellectuals who discuss the issue of homosexual clergy in print range from those who urge acceptance to those who believe that even celibate homosexuals should not be ordained. Many conservative Protestant churches view all homosexual behavior as sinful and preclude sexually active homosexuals from ministry. At the other end, gay churches exist which minister directly to homosexuals through a gay clergy.

Chapter 8 addresses issues related to homosexuality and the culture of celibacy. The points raised there apply to religious denominations that do not require celibacy from their heterosexual ministers but do require it from homosexual ones. Here we want to touch on a few points regarding the personal development of homosexual self-identity in ministry and the challenges this creates for therapy.

As distinguished above, homosexual or lesbian behavior may emerge in several contexts. These include: (1) the process of personal discovery of one's sexual orientation; (2) searching for a committed partner; (3) during an impulsive, unreflected upon emotional experience in which the person gets "carried away," and (4) in the context of compulsive, totally unintegrated acting out behavior. The therapeutic task will vary in each case with the approaches outlined above and in chapter 8, which depend on the individual context as to whether or not they are relevant. The therapeutic task in each case is to contextualize the meaning of focusing on homosexuality as a personal growth issue in order to develop appropriate goals.

We want to highlight a critical cultural issue in light of the normative heterosexual filter of the majority culture. The social taboos that prevent homosexuals or lesbians from easily finding a supportive social milieu conducive to resolving developmental issues applies doubly for the minister engaged in that journey. Many of the social outlets are of a problematic nature for clergy: gay bars, sexually oriented entertainments, etc. The lack of social freedom impedes the efficiency of this development and it often proceeds at an agonizingly slow pace. It is difficult to self-explore when, by definition, exploration is disapproved. We remember a similar notion from psychologist

Gerald Davison (1976) who pointed out the absurdity of viewing homosexuality as an emotional disorder. Davison asks us to imagine a society in which anxiety is illegal. Imagine, further, the turmoil of persons who experience anxiety. In this scenario the anxious person is emotionally bound up in never expressing the anxiety and living in terror that others will find him out. Such an environment would make it highly unlikely that one could do the necessary work to cope with anxiety.

Discovering appropriate social outlets that will enable the client to sort out his or her sexual orientation issues is tricky. The recovering alcoholic may actually have an advantage here. One of the most therapeutic experiences for gay clergy who are also alcoholic is participation in gay AA. In gay AA members can freely express their feelings about two of the most important realities in their life, their drinking problem and their sexuality. For conflicted religious professionals this represents the first time they get to know at a personal level intelligent gay men and women who openly discuss topics such as integrating spirituality with recovery. In this atmosphere we have witnessed literally hundreds of gay clergy develop a self-understanding that for the first time leads to open acceptance of their sexual orientation. At the same time this discussion takes place in a social context of seriousness about recovery. Relationships are not entered into in the manner of the bar scene and decisions for sexual abstinence receive respect.

For those who are not recovering alcoholics ready-made and appropriate forums are harder to locate. Some churches have gay-oriented special interest gatherings which may serve the same purpose. Not all of these groups receive official support from the church body and often function as an underground church. Although helpful, they lack the full acceptance of the broader community. This community acceptance is crucial for research indicates that support from heterosexual friends is highly associated with self-acceptance for homosexuals.

Obtaining that support raises the important issue of "coming out" with its advantages and disadvantages. Coming out has emerged as a political issue within the gay community. Some emphasize individual discretion in whether or not to come out and with whom. Others maintain that remaining closeted impairs the freedom of the total community and empowers external discrimination to grow into self-discrimination and self-hatred. Coming out, in this view, is an act of political freedom for the gay community as well as the individual. Some go so far as to engage in the involuntary public "outing" of closeted gay men and women.

Since therapists have persons not politics as their primary responsibility we should assist our gay clients to reflect carefully upon consequences of coming out. Discrimination against gays, particularly in church settings, may constitute occupational suicide to one who comes out publicly. What is the downside from a full public disclosure? Is it worth the negative consequences? What resources does the person have to cope with the resulting stress? Could he or she survive financially? Emotionally?

In our experience many gay ministers, sisters, and brothers choose to come out selectively. They hand pick family, friends, or colleagues to whom they reveal their sexual orientation. This often solves the dilemma of obtaining support from the broader community without at the same time jeopardizing their entire careers. Even this process is often precarious for the client. Many agonize over telling family members. Clinicians who are experienced in working with gay clients on developmental issues will notice how the same developmental issues with gay clergy carry a delay from a few years to decades. More and more we see young gay men and women coming out in their late teens and certainly by their midtwenties. With clergy, sisters, and brothers this public acknowledgment is quite selective at these same ages and will likely remain selective for the majority.

This is not surprising when we consider the institutional messages gay clergy receive. President Clinton galvanized national debate on the issue of gays in the military when he instituted the infamous, "Don't ask, don't tell" policy. Most churches had this policy down to a science long ago. At a workshop on sexual issues for clergy we heard a liberal Catholic moral theologian report that he advises Catholic seminarians never to share their sexual orientation with anyone, not even fellow seminarians. Aside from flying in the face of research about self-acceptance, this advice ignores any understanding of the interpersonal nature of self-identity. It implies that people develop self-understanding in isolation from social feedback.

We propose assisting clients in selective coming out when they choose that goal. Traditional therapeutic strategies may assist this process such as cognitive restructuring for imagined catastrophes or role-playing to develop scripts for the dialogues. Frequently we observe that the gay person, whether male or female, will first discuss their sexual orientation with a woman. Research and clinical experience indicate that women are less likely to be homophobic. Often we help the client select a supportive female friend or relative, a sister, sister-in-law, or colleague. We would all like to have the proverbial dollar for each encounter that ends up with the confidant saying, "I already knew." When these first encounters end successfully, the task shifts to selecting a slightly less certain person to come out to, and so on until the person has the skill to be open as he or she chooses.

Selective coming out is not a magic elixir for coping with a gay orientation in ministry but it provides a supportive environment where people can be themselves and discuss the whole range of human concerns that are most important to them.

8.

Celibacy

Celibacy is associated today with ordination or being a nun, monk, or brother in the Roman Catholic tradition. The commitment to lifelong celibacy means that priests, nuns, and male members of religious orders forgo having a spouse, must abstain from sexual intercourse, and avoid those acts that may lead to genital intimacy.

Although there are those both within and outside contemporary Roman Catholicism who would like to separate the link between ordination/vowed religious life and celibacy, this connection continues to be a fact of life for those wishing to follow these vocational callings in this church. As a result, how Catholic celibate ministers come to grips with their own sexuality does have a crucial impact on their overall lives and ministry.

COUNTERTRANSFERENCE

Due to the controversial nature of celibacy, its relatively long (though recently questioned) tradition in the modern Roman Catholic Church, and its countercultural nature today, countertransference among therapists who work with this population often occurs when celibacy is dealt with in treatment. For instance, those from a Roman Catholic tradition sometimes experience an unconscious or even observable impetus to keep the

163

person on the "straight and narrow" by having them remain celibate. This is evidenced when the therapist focuses on the issue of scandal should acting-out behavior become known. It is also present when the therapist expends a great deal of energy on "preventing temptation" rather than helping the person understand the dynamics of why the person is avoiding celibate living and how he or she feels about this behavior.

These countertransferences are sometimes encouraged by church authorities who send the celibate minister to the therapist and who are responsible for paying for the treatment. The message given the therapist is: "They are not living as celibates. They have made a promise to be celibate. Help them to see the error of their ways and live up to their promise or we will have to remove them from ministry."

From the point of view of the church authorities this stand may seem quite reasonable. However, to the therapist naturally, the key issue here is not proper behavior but "understanding." Consequently, some of the essential therapeutic questions are: Does the person have a good level of self-understanding? What is the level of sexual development present? How has intimacy been negotiated in the past and is it being confronted in interpersonal situations now? When the person made the commitment to be celibate, was he or she mature enough to make this commitment? And, if no, can and do they wish to recommit at this point?

This last question is a key one because, as in marriage, original commitment is largely made in the unconscious for an array of reasons, both mature and immature. The fact that one made a decision early in life or for immature reasons is only part of the issue in exploring this area. (After all, how many therapists entered their field of endeavor for questionable reasons, such as power, personal unresolved issues, etc.?) The important element here is for the clients to allow the mature reasons and questions to rise to the surface now, to put aside the immature ones of early conditioning in life, and to look at their decision again and again.

Celibacy, as in the case of sexual development in general, looks different when it is examined at various points in the life of the ordained or vowed Catholic minister. For instance, a young seminarian who is homosexual in orientation may have suppressed his sexuality as a way of avoiding (in his words) "complications" in life, given the Church and his parents' perceived stand against homosexuality.

When he is in his early twenties, if he has even a fleeting genital encounter with another seminarian this may result in panic, further suppression, and a general avoidance of the issue as long as this is possible. He may bring it to confession, be counseled to avoid the person in question, and to remember his vows.

However, this same seminarian after he is ordained and in ministry for several years will probably not respond in the same way. Since ordination he will have met many more people, been subjected to the pressures of ministry, and be in greater need to broach the issue of intimacy, sexuality, and his own orientation. As one seminarian I once asked about celibacy said, "I really feel I don't have time to deal with that issue now. I am overwhelmed with all of the other identity issues surrounding the role of priesthood." Later, after he had resolved many of these issues in therapy, he made a decision to take a leave from the seminary to face the questions that naturally surround a commitment to being celibate for life. The timing at that point was correct for him to do this.

In another case, a person who as a seminarian avoided looking at his own sexuality, found that as a priest he could no longer do this because his wall of avoidance was being broken down by strong impulses to have brief sexual encounters in the gym. When he came in because of this crisis, the timing was right for him to look at his identity as a whole, discuss his orientation with close friends and family (which had been previously considered too dangerous), and to make a decision to leave and move in with a gay partner so he could be fully and freely who he felt he was.

Countertransference, which prevents an openness on the therapist's part to help celibate ministers to look clearly at themselves as sexual persons at each stage of development, then will prevent a responsiveness to the needs of such patients at this time in their lives. Consequently, sensitivity to this type of obstructionism because of the therapist's own religious background or in response to pressures from religious authorities needs to be present.

On the other end of the continuum is a more common type of countertransference. It is the unspoken belief on the part of the therapist that: "Celibacy is unnatural and the root of *all* the problems of the celibate minister." When this occurs, the therapist indirectly, or, once again, sometimes quite directly, urges the patient to claim what the therapist believes is a more wholesome experience of sexuality. In this case, the therapist might encourage either a style of life that includes "winking" at the vows and having a genital relationship on the side, or, believing that such vows are impossible to keep, might suggest that the person must leave ministry within the Church if he or she is ever to become whole.

Instead, celibacy (as in the case of any value) needs to be explored in the therapy with openness and a desire to see how it can help those in treatment to understand their thoughts and feelings about it as well as the actions they have taken in life because, or in spite, of it. The point being made here is that both healthy and unhealthy styles of living are possible for the celibate minister. The role of the therapist is to help the person understand where they are on the continuum in terms of health in this area. And so, with this in mind, insight is the obvious goal, and therapists must be sensitive to possible "therapist coercion" in either direction, especially since celibacy is so central to the therapy of Roman Catholic celibate ministers.

THE CENTRALITY OF CELIBACY IN THE THERAPY

The authors have found that healthy, happy celibate living is possible. However, it is not a once-and-for-all decision but rather one which requires renegotiation and recommitment again and again in life. Furthermore, because sexuality, self-image, and relationship are intertwined, celibacy and sexuality are often the center stages upon which many other issues are played out in life.

Self-esteem, for instance, may be a problem early in life and throughout adolescence but finally come to the fore for a celibate in early adulthood. At this point he or she has more opportunities to enter into interpersonal arenas which were previously unavailable.

An example of this is a religious brother in his midtwenties who is a high school teacher. Up to this point in his life he had not had much opportunity to interact with women his age. In addition, when an opportunity occurred, he reported that they were not really interested in him since he was "a nerd of sorts."

However, when he decided to pursue graduate study he had an opportunity to interact with women his own age who had never married or were divorced. When one of the women in his class built a friendship with him, he felt his self-esteem and confidence increase and began seriously to consider the possibility of a relationship. Although it did not develop into one with this person, he kept this possibility in mind and eventually did meet someone and left religious life one year later.

The decision to leave ministry in the Roman Catholic tradition can involve people from early to late middle age, or older. As a matter of fact, the number of instances of people who have left late in life is surprising.

While the reasons for leaving religious life, especially for men, are diverse, some patterns appear to be emerging based on clinical material. These include:

1. An inability to be vulnerable to other persons and to build lasting affective relationships during their years of ministry.
2. A tendency to be distant and cognitive.
3. The move to leave is triggered by a trauma (sickness, loss of position/role of respect) or major change in life (retirement).
4. A belief that this was the last chance they had to have a significant companion in life.
5. An underdeveloped need for approval by their peers in the Church.

So, no matter what the age of the celibate minister, a good deal of information can be gleaned about the person's psychosexual development by providing them with time to explore their appreciation of and commitment to celibacy at this point in their lives.

ASEXUALITY AND HEALTHY SEXUALITY

Since sexuality is at the core of anyone's life, then helping ministers to see how they are living as sexual persons is usually an essential part of the overall treatment plan. Given that, it would be helpful to see some of the elements present in those who have embraced celibacy as part of their vocation and are living this way in a healthy fashion.

In addition, some of the major styles of nonacceptance of celibacy on the part of those still publicly committed to the vow are also worth noting so that discussion with patients about this area is possible. First, however, it would be helpful to review briefly a pattern that mimics healthy celibacy: asexuality.

Asexuality

For our purposes here, the "healthy celibate" group includes those persons who are neither asexual nor engaged in genital behavior on an ongoing basis but are leading a generally fulfilling interpersonal life. Since asexual behavior sometimes mimics healthy celibacy, the celibate style of interacting and celibate ministers' attitudes toward intimacy need to be examined closely to determine if the individual is aware of their own sexuality and has come to terms with it or if they have ignored, minimized, or suppressed sexual impulses, conflicts, and experiences.

Asexual individuals often tend not to present as problems to others in ministry because they are chronically nice in their interactions. In these cases the focus of the person's life is primarily on the activity of ministry as well as living up to an image of what he or she feels a religious should be. Presenting a "loving face" is seen as a real value. Conflict, and the deep form of intimacy and communication that often comes with it, are usually absent.

Amongst asexual individuals, quite different in nature is one who has an unpleasant character style. This is the very angry and self-righteous individual who has put his or her sexuality on hold either consciously or unconsciously and interpersonally terrorizes the world because of it. Because of a lack of awareness, this type often avoids treatment, and if he or she enters it the reason is either because of pressure from authority or because of feeling worn down by the consequences of such inappropriate behavior.

These asexual patterns are familiar in the seminary and early formation years of celibate ministers, until a realization is triggered that something very important (sexuality) has been held back in the person's life. The triggers to such an awareness can be a sexual overture by someone, a feeling of deep dissatisfaction regarding present levels of intimacy with others, or counseling or spiritual guidance which raises questions and feelings about one's sexuality and sexual development. Until such an examination takes place, though, "healthy celibacy," and all this label implies, are usually absent.

Healthy Celibacy

For our purposes here, the "healthy celibate" is:

Self-aware;
Appreciative of his or her own sexual orientation;
Able to be intimate and value such closeness;
Has an ability to learn from interpersonal interaction;
Is able to see sexuality as part of the spiritual–faith dimension of the life of the minister rather than being something to suppress or cut off from one's life.

Good self-awareness is essential for a person who is a committed celibate who also wants to be someone who is mature and emotionally healthy. Otherwise, seductive behavior, misogyny, compulsive homo/heterophobic behavior might well be the result. Therapy is a wonderful place for a person to speak about sexuality, sexual orientation, perceived "failings" as a celibate, and troublesome forms of interpersonal behavior. Since the therapy setting is open, welcoming, and not bound by the rubrics of other church-related guidance settings, which may not provide the time or impetus, or (maybe even more importantly) the freedom to share openly on topics of a psychological nature (e.g., confession or the sacrament of reconciliation as it is now called), it is an ideal place for new exploration of self-awareness and acceptance to take place. (This incidentally may be one of the major reasons why many new candidates for priesthood or religious life choose to enter therapy as part of their initial formation experience for ministry.)

Self-awareness involves knowing what and how one feels about sexual issues and persons in one's life and to be aware of the difference between a desire and an action. When this does not occur, the person will either screen out his or her feelings until they present themselves in a possibly overwhelming way or they may not realize the difference between experiencing a feeling and acting upon it.

Having the opportunity to be honest about one's feelings can be the linchpin to understanding them in a way that is helpful for growth and decisions.

> For instance, in one case a young seminarian told the therapist that the older adolescents in the school where he taught had very muscular bodies which were naturally very attractive to him given his homosexual orientation. This led to a discussion of his sexual history, dating experiences with other males of his age, intimacy he now had which he felt was appropriate, and how he avoided crossing appropriate boundaries, and getting sexually involved with his students.
>
> Though the students were only 6 years younger than he in some cases, he was able to see some of the problems which would result if he acted upon his impulses. In addition, he was able to open up new lines of communication with others his age, examine his own sexuality, and finally reach a point where he could decide that he would not be able to live a celibate life.

In another case, where the opportunity for such discussion with a therapist did not take place, the impulses were kept in and not discussed, others with homosexual orientation inside and outside of the ministry were avoided, and frustration built up and was dealt with through excessive drinking and anonymous sexual encounters at the gym. Finally, on one occasion, after having a good deal of alcohol to drink, the priest genitally fondled a young man whom he had just met, and was reported to the police for indecent assault. Part of the treatment for this priest would probably include opportunities for him to speak about his sexuality and impulses as well as Gay AA and opportunities to interact with adults of his own orientation. However, the negative consequence of his acting out behavior in this instance might have been avoided if he had previously been able to deal in therapy with his impulses and see the vast difference between desire and action. In another instance of poor self-awareness, the celibate minister involved slowly developed a relationship with a woman who had previously been intimate with another priest. He did not understand that she had been in an abusive situation and needed a great deal of support and clear limits to build up trust in order to help her deal with other issues in her own life. In cases like these, the person feels he is just responding to another's needs as well as satisfying his own. Yet, this rationalization can lead to harm for both parties.

The following suggestion given to therapists obviously can also be given to persons in ministry as well: "You should never do anything with someone who is your client (parishioner, student, spiritual directee) that you would not be willing to describe out loud in front of your colleagues." However, unlike therapy, which often has supervision built in (though as we can see in the example of patient abuse cases this can be circumvented as well), there is little assistance in this area to help the person in ministry know which relationships are more apt to lead to inappropriate behavior on the part of the minister and which aren't.

Awareness and an appreciation of one's own sexual orientation is also present in healthy celibate ministers. In the case of a heterosexually oriented person, awareness of one's orientation is rarely a problem. However, prizing one's sexuality may be. As a result, when interviewing someone who is celibate it is important to have them talk about their own past sexual history, present levels of interaction with others with whom they are intimate, their views on autoerotic behavior such as masturbation, and how they would describe healthy sexual behavior for both celibates and noncelibates.

Problems arise more in this area with respect to being gay or bisexual. Men and women with either of these two sexual orientations may well have either avoided coming to grips with such a view of themselves or feel if it is their orientation, that it is "bad" and must be eliminated or lessened in some way.

Society and organized religion unfortunately often support this view, thus adding credence to their inappropriate, exaggerated, negative self-image with respect to their sexuality. This may become more and more of a unique problem in the Roman Catholic Church if there is a marked increase in the percentage of gay seminarians and priests, which some feel is the case today. (We have no definite statistics other than qualitative impressions by some whose clinical practice includes significant numbers of priests and seminarians.)

To discover the person's appreciation of his or her own orientation, therapy should include an exploration of both the patient's fantasy objects and past sexual behavior that includes but is not limited to actual dating. (Dating those of the opposite gender for the sake of appearances, or due to a belief that this is what one should do no matter what one's impulses are, is common developmentally for this group.)

Being able to be intimate and value closeness, as well as to learn from intimacy with others, is also another sign of a healthy celibate. In such cases, persons who say they are celibate are in fact not involved in genital behavior with others. However, they are able to be physically affectionate without being either seductive or scrupulous, are able to be personally vulnerable and open themselves up emotionally, and are able to accept both love and criticism.

Without such closeness present, there is a real absence of both the ability to love others in a way that reflects much of the person's own true feelings and needs. In addition, when healthy intimacy is absent, it often leads the person to focus more on things (rites, rituals, hobbies) or other quests (power, accomplishment) in such a way as to continue a delay in personal, interpersonal, and sexual development.

PASSIVE CELIBACY

Since the decision to live as a celibate is an intentional step, the therapist has to be aware of those patients who have unconsciously or consciously not made such a commitment. To help clients see this in the context of the treatment would be a very helpful way to demonstrate the need for clarity and responsibility. Passive celibacy as it is being termed here by the authors refers to persons whose public life-style as a Catholic priest, nun, or religious proclaims them as celibate. Yet, they still seem to be open to a genital relationship if it occurs. In cases such as these, this openness can be understood by the person and justified in a number of ways. On the other hand, it may be a stance that is not realized at the time the person comes into therapy and only as reflection, summarization, and other types of interpretation take place do they begin to recognize this pattern of behavior on their part and question their own unresolved issues surrounding celibacy.

Conscious passive celibacy, as in all sexual patterns, can occur among persons who are homosexual, heterosexual, or bisexual. To illustrate here, a homosexual male will be used as an example.

In the following case the priest has long come to grips with his homosexuality, accepts it, and prizes his orientation although he admits it would be a lot easier for him in the world if he were heterosexual. When asked if he wants to be celibate and refrain from genital behavior, he responds in the negative. He says he would like to remain a priest because he loves the ministry but that he also wants to be in a significant relationship with another man that will include genital contact.

When asked how he has come to this decision given his publicly proclaimed position as a celibate priest he responds by saying he has decided to be "chaste but not celibate." As in any area of the therapy, he is naturally questioned further as to what he means by this, and he says that he will be loyal to one person, which he considers a "chaste" life, but not be celibate. When questioned further about this change in approach to his commitment as a priest he gives the following reasons why he has decided to make a shift:

1. He feels as a person he is entitled to intimacy and that he can no longer remain celibate. He feels if he tries to do so, it will result in a very lonely existence or produce spurts of acting out behavior at the gym or bar which could be physically dangerous and wouldn't be interpersonally fulfilling.
2. He does not feel guilty because he sees celibacy as a "church law" which has not always been in effect and points out that other denominations do not have such a silly rule.
3. He believes he will be a better priest because in the past when he was in a relationship with other seminarians or priests during his seminary years, he was more enthusiastic, peaceful, and productive.

When asked the downside of his decision, as in the case of looking at any behavior that one has decided to do privately, there is the expected hesitation accompanied by an attempt to minimize the potential problems. For instance, he goes on to say that he realizes that if it came to light it might cause scandal but he doubts whether anyone would ever find out. In addition, he gives examples of a number of other gay priests who are in relationships and doing quite well in their ministry.

He bolsters his position by citing instances of heterosexual relationships among priests. If pushed further as to what he would do if it came to light and he were removed by the bishop from the priesthood, bravado often occurs accompanied by anger against the system, especially the bishop.

There is a danger at this point for the therapist to be pulled into the hypothetical argument, either on the side of the patient or on the side of the diocese, neither of which is helpful. To see the patient's comments as but a further indication in the therapist's mind that celibacy is foolish and to collaborate with him in an effort to circumvent the system, fails to open up the potential consequences of this behavior. Such consequences include: being ejected from the priesthood; receiving negative responses from parishioners, family, colleagues, and friends; the stress of living a double life.

Trying to force the situation to a point of closure by having the priest decide either to embrace celibacy as a priest or leave, is also a mistake in judgment. Once the issues of the duplicity and consequences and a full history of sexual–interpersonal development has been laid before the patient, the decision is clearly his to make. As in all psychotherapy, insight into the behavior is the goal so the patient can decide what, how, and when to take action. Exploration in this area is to help the patient understand his or her psychosexual development and how this is impacting their actions.

An indirect but difficult part of conscious passive celibacy is the compulsive nature it takes in some cases. In such instances there is an inordinate focus on obtaining a significant relationship before "it is too late." The fear at this point is of growing old and unattractive, passing the time when one can find a partner, or in the case of heterosexual women, passing the time when getting pregnant and having children is possible.

When this stress is present it affects perspective dramatically; and anxiety and anhedonia may result, and there may be overpowering intrusive behavior with those they view as potential mates. The situation is made even worse in those instances when it occurs between two persons (celibate or not) who are experiencing the same stress or are sexually immature.

For instance, in the setting of spiritual direction, mentoring, or religious counseling, trust might be built up to the point where the person coming for help is able to examine their desires and impulses. In the process, positive transference may take place because of the feelings of freedom that have come to the fore once the person has been given encouragement to self-explore without fear of negative judgment.

In such instances, if the person providing the guidance is also having problems with issues around celibacy, and responds to the transference as he or she would other sexual nontransferential overtures with a consenting adult outside of the counseling session, naturally problems will result for both parties involved in the interaction. For "passive celibates" one of the real problems is failure to recognize boundaries, and a failure to realize the implications of any active sexual behavior with counselees, parishioners, employees, or even colleagues when the relationship hasn't been fully discussed and is one that is among equals.

Unconscious Passive Celibacy

Unconscious passive celibacy takes place when a person has extensive experiences in acting out genitally with a partner or partners, but still denies that he or she is really not living a celibate life. By this I don't mean that if one becomes physically close to another individual through fondling, passionate kissing, or even intercourse on one or two occasions, that the person is not living a primarily celibate existence. Since there is a natural tendency to want to develop a relationship in a way in which the genital is included, this may well happen during the course of the vocational life of a celibate.

What is being pointed to here are those instances when Catholic priests, nuns, or brothers have an ongoing pattern of acting out which they don't claim responsibility for, but rather see as unavoidable, impulsive, or limited occurrences. The goal in such instances is not of course to be involved in assigning blame. Rather, the aim is to examine the rationalizations for what they are, so clients can understand and claim responsibility for their behavior and thereby avoid unexpected negative consequences. Whether the behavior is shrouded in defenses or not, the results can nevertheless still be devastating. The old Chinese proverb, "In nature there are no rewards and punishments, only consequences," must be appreciated here by both the therapist and patient.

An example of this is the nun who gets physically involved with priests with whom she interacts as colleagues or friends, and then claims: "Oh, it just got out of control; I didn't expect things would go that far." Another is the priest who is a spiritual guide to laypeople and nuns, and then when he finds one attractive and vulnerable, begins to remove the boundaries that should be there, as in therapy, with the excuse: "I don't know what overcame me," or, "It didn't hurt anything. She needed someone close to her at that point." A key goal for treatment should be the progressive removal of repression, denial, avoidance, and inappropriate belief systems.

A final example of passive celibacy is the inadequate person in ministry who finds him- or herself in a transferential position of power which provides access to a broader range of friends or acquaintances. Unfortunately, in seminaries and formation programs, little is said about transference and countertransference. As a result, persons in ministry are in a dangerous position to act on the positive transference received by attempting to become or becoming physically intimate with persons they are interacting with in the parish/religious institution.

This is dangerous for both partners. In the case of the parishioner, the result of a trust broken can be devastating. Even in those cases where the parishioner was testing the limits (possibly because the limits in the past weren't there and he or she was desperately looking for a place in which to be safe), the avoidable harm done by the minister (be the person a priest, brother, sister, or married minister in the instance of a noncelibate), can be tremendous.

In the case of the ministers, they may be setting themselves up for a terrible situation where their whole life's work can be quickly compromised. The therapist's goal in any behavior, including the sexual, is to help the patient understand it so his or her own level of development can be appreciated and unnecessary acting out avoided. Demonstrating patterns and helping the person understand the forms of transference and countertransference that are common in ministry are essential as part of the treatment.

HOMOSEXUALITY DISCOVERED AND EMBRACED AS A SEXUAL ORIENTATION BY THE CELIBATE

Sometimes in seminaries and houses of formation for priests, nuns, and brothers, a latently gay person is given the opportunity by another similarly oriented person to express behavior that is appropriate to his or her own orientation but which has been hitherto repressed, denied, or avoided. When this occurs, a number of difficulties can arise. These include:

1. An intense love affair that doesn't include the opportunity for reflection and integration of the experience.

2. Panic which results in continued avoidance of reflection on one's sexual identity.
3. The development of a "dual life" which may cause guilt, stress, or undue anxiety, leading to a decision regarding one's life vocation that may be premature.
4. Acting-out behavior that is never confronted.

In the case of the intense love affair that doesn't include the opportunity for reflection, the person adopts an adolescentlike approach to the relationship. There is an intensity and focus on the other person involved which excludes others in the house with whom he or she is living, as well as sometimes inducing a markedly reduced interest in the work at hand.

The only one the person feels free to share feelings about the relationship with is the other person involved. This gives the other person a great deal of power, especially if he or she has had gay experiences before and is more comfortable or confident with their identity. This may lead to subtle manipulation of the weaker person. It also may lead to a premature decision to leave religious life or the priesthood.

Naturally, another problem that may arise which the person in this situation must deal with is the attitude of other seminarians, sisters, or brothers in formation (depending on the situation) who feel he or she is being too exclusive in this relationship and is also not living up to the vow of celibacy. Consequently, former friends and confidants may move out of the circle of support and become difficult to deal with. This will serve to push the inexperienced loner further into the physical and psychological "arms" of the other person or force him or her to decide to return to a faithfulness to the vow of celibacy.

When the latter occurs, a great deal of stress between the partners takes place, even when both tacitly agree that this would be a good thing for both of them. What often happens is that one of the partners, often the more experienced of the two, raises a loyalty conflict. This is done by asking of the less experienced partner: "Who is first in your life, me or your celibate vocation to the priesthood or vowed religious life?" (whichever is the case in this instance).

If this conflict can be negotiated, then a strong friendship may be possible. However, even when it is, often one of the two will repeatedly test the limits again when the two of them are together and move toward genital contact. Since it is natural for the other person to be stimulated and want to be involved on that level, compromises are made again and again until one or both finally draw back.

In many cases though, the relationship cannot be renegotiated once one partner refuses to engage in genital intimacy. The result is a complete break, and a hurt, angry scene which precipitates a final split. This then often results in one of the partners who feels rejected seeking another partner for genital contact, and the one who drew back seeking intimate but non-genital friendships or withdrawing for a period of time into having only distant relationships with others.

The therapist's role in this process is to aid the person being treated (whether the more or less experienced partner) to understand the dynamics of the interaction and to help them both understand and take responsibility for their part in it. This may take a period of time since projection will be strong as a way of warding off personal narcissistic injury. Unfortunately, if this blaming of the other continues as a way of supporting personal, tenuous self-esteem, then the pattern will repeat itself again and again.

At the other end of the spectrum, the situation can also reach a danger point if the more experienced partner decides to pull back in the relationship. The person who is less experienced and not in a position to readily share going through a dashed first love affair (as is age appropriate in adolescence), may fall into a deep depression. Suicidal impulses or dramatic gestures to draw attention to their plight may occur and may sadly be miscalculated, leading to the person's desired or accidental death. Consequently, mental health professionals must be involved with persons close to or responsible for their clients who are in this situation.

Panic is another possible result when people experience their homosexuality in a genital way for the first time. Because of society's negative attitudes, the person may have hidden away or rationalized homosexual impulses. In addition, church authorities and formal or informal teachings cause problems for a homosexual designated leader who is a member of a mainline religion.

This panic will be lessened when a therapist is in a position to guide the individual to an understanding of his or her own sexual development. In such a setting, the person can see that an orientation is not an aberration but a physical given that needs to be understood, prized, and then integrated in such a way that the person can either choose a celibate or genitally active life-style.

Another difficulty when a homosexually oriented person has previously denied or repressed his or her sexual identity and has a genital experience which is not fully discussed or understood, is the development of a "dual life" or unbridled acting out behavior (promiscuity). When people lead a supposedly committed celibate life on the surface and have secret, consistent genital interactions with one or more people, this may cause a great deal of guilt, stress, or undue anxiety leading to a splitting off of the affect with respect to this life-style or a premature decision to leave religious life.

This was seen especially in the 1960s in the Catholic Church after Vatican II. During this period many people left the priesthood and their religious vocations. No doubt many really needed to do this and gave adequate reflection to this step. Others, however, failed to realize that "falling in love" or more aptly "falling in love with falling in love" (experiencing the high of an intense relationship) need not void one's celibate vocation. Yet, some left who are now unhappy about it because insufficient time was spent at the time in reflection and processing the situation.

Acting out behavior also can occur when reflection is absent. This is dangerous not only because of the physical danger of AIDS and venereal diseases but also because of the psychological hazards of inadequate psychosexual identity formation. This includes an appreciation of all the aspects of intimacy and relationship and the possibility of triggering a sexually addictive style which then becomes quite difficult to treat.

SITUATIONAL HOMOSEXUALITY

In single-sex environments situational homosexuality or lesbianism is not uncommon. Due to the lack of available heterosexual partners, homosexual or lesbian behavior occurs in individuals who under other circumstances would prefer a heterosexual partner. In the case of educational-formation settings for Catholic clergy and religious, questions have often been raised as to whether this also occurs and what to do when it does.

Although there are no statistics on it, clinically, the authors have noted that the occurrence of situational homosexuality or lesbianism is less than sensational stories would have us believe. In addition, there is a gender difference which is notable.

In seminaries, whereas the presence today of a high percentage of homosexually oriented persons is in evidence, there is little evidence of rampant situational homosexuality. A number of hypotheses may be posited for this:

1. The male psychology which deemphasizes affiliation and emphasizes separation and individuation.
2. The appropriation of a clear sense of one's sexual orientation as heterosexual prior to entering the seminary or religious life.
3. The psychological taboo against homosexual behavior by many heterosexual males.
4. The presence of an "incest taboo" that operates in shared communal settings such as kibbutz or gender-integrated college dormitories.

In the case of a setting for women the issue is not as clear. Due to an expressed value and greater appreciation for affiliation, more ease in having physical contact with members of the same sex, as well as a more developed appreciation for their own affective world, situational sexuality appears somewhat common in female single-sex religious settings. No empirical study, to date, exists on this topic.

When it does occur, however, the nun may seek counseling around whether or not she is a lesbian. As in the case of those coming from other vocational settings, the therapist calmly and clearly explores the person's fantasies and history to help the individual attain clarity. It is a great opportunity to help the person understand herself on a number of levels.

For instance, a comment-question such as: "It seems as you describe the possibility of being lesbian, you get somewhat agitated. Suppose a person did find out she was lesbian in orientation, what would be the terrible thing about that?" Even in the case of women who aren't lesbian in orientation a question such as this can open up women to their own prejudices, fears, and homophobic tendencies.

If the person's fantasies and history point to a heterosexual orientation, then exploration of the interpersonal needs and desires of the individual becomes important. Situational sexuality is not so important because persons have genital contact with someone of the same sex as it obviously is notable for the needs they are trying to fulfill through such interactions. And so, the overt concerns which brought the person into treatment can be an opportunity, once they are clarified and lessened, to explore and help provide insight into an array of human development issues should the client desire to do so when offered this option.

SOME FINAL COMMENTS ON CELIBACY AND THERAPY

Exploring the interpersonal development of a person within the context of how he or she lives with respect to celibacy can lead to a great amount of helpful information for the patient. Not only will it help the patient to better understand legitimate needs, dangerous impulses, and interpersonal style, it will also guide him or her in making intelligent decisions about the future.

A nun who was sexually abused early in life may have gone into the convent to be safe. As she explores her life now in light of knowing this, she may feel that despite this she is willing and desirous of making a more mature and informed recommitment to religious life now. On the other hand, she may wish to take a leave of absence (generally referred to as going on a period of exclaustration, which is renewable each year for a period of 3 years) to be in a position to interact more freely with others. However, by examining her sexual life, such an informed decision becomes possible.

Also, when someone violates the rule of celibacy and is involved in genital intimacy with another person, this too is an opportunity for examination of one's sexual and interpersonal life. When done in the context of therapy, the relationships can be looked at with candor and openness which will help the person avoid taking a step that may not be mature or necessary.

For instance, if a nun has a relationship which involves intercourse or what she describes as "heavy petting," this may not mean that she has lost her vocation. The experience of being in a romantic relationship might even help her to understand how to love others more deeply and thus improve her ministry and strengthen her vocation.

The trauma of "falling in love," even when it does not involve physical intimacy, can of course cause the person to ride an emotional roller-coaster, but the point being made is that when guided in therapy it need not lead to problems which impair a person's vocation should there be a desire to stay. Also, if the person does decide to leave ministry, the therapy can provide a setting in which to examine both the benefits and drawbacks of marriage with the person with whom he or she may be involved.

Moreover, just as an archaic superego can keep a person inappropriately tied to celibacy and religious life, it can be the push behind a person making a decision to marry which in the end is of no benefit to either party involved. So, the advantages of therapy are potentially quite great when someone is looking at their own sexual identity and how it is being nourished or limited in the context of a celibate vocation to ministry.

PART IV

Observing Limits and Handling Change

In this section we address issues related to the thorny problem in ministry of maintaining appropriate boundaries as well as adapting to the myriad transitions that are part and parcel of the ministry life-style. Particularly in the area of boundary maintenance, therapists will note that assumptions and rules of conduct about socializing that protect client welfare in the counseling field cannot apply directly to ministry. This provides both hazards and opportunities for ministers and, to be helpful, therapists must be aware of the subtle and not so subtle cultural distinctions.

9.

Boundaries and Transitions

DUAL RELATIONSHIPS: THE SCOPE OF THE PROBLEM

In the helping professions the principle of dual relationships forms the backbone for discerning the ethics of many an entangled relationship. Helpers, whether they are physicians, nurses, or therapists, are to avoid nonprofessional relationships with clients as much as possible, and never, never personally benefit from inadvertent or unavoidable ones. Closely allied to this principle, if somewhat broader, is the ancient formula embedded in the Hippocratic oath that one should, "First, do no harm." Dual relationships have an inherent propensity to harm the client. The helper who begins to value the client for the stock tips she can provide, the lonely therapist going through a painful divorce who feels supported and nurtured by a client, these are situations that increase the probability of treatment exploitation.

Out of the need to prevent harmful, entangled situations, the ethical maxim of observing boundaries has emerged to guide professionals in their relationships. When they violate boundaries they not only harm clients, they weaken the integrity of the profession and cause the public to view them with mistrust. In the case of psychotherapy, for example, loss of trust would render the entire therapeutic enterprise unattainable.

Trust is equally critical within the field of pastoral care. When the public views the clergy as untrustworthy, clergy will no longer have an effective healing environment for ministry. At present, as national polls indicate, clergy do have public trust. Despite media reports of notorious sexual scandals involving pedophilia, the public continues to admire clergy more than most professional groups, including psychologists.

If therapists attempt to translate directly our concepts of boundaries and dual relationships into guidelines for the religious professional, we will misunderstand an important reality of the clerical culture. Boundaries and limits, and by implication dual relationships, are not metaphors that drive the culture of service for ministers. As one pastor told us, "The Gospel sees the pastor as one who goes beyond boundaries to serve others." The image of Jesus as the Good Shepherd who leaves 99 saved to search for the one lost, is the emotionally rich metaphor that inspires ministers. By contrast, boundaries, limits, and dual relationships sound insipid and legalistic.

Dual relationships are at the heart of most religious professionals' lives. They share meals, attend family celebrations, purchase services, bury friends, argue policy, and play tennis with the same people they lead in worship, help solve ethical dilemmas, and whose confessions they hear. While the mental health professional can easily create boundaries by drawing a line in an appointment book, the minister's social and personal reality is spatially fluid. Ministers are more apt to identify with the Gospel story of Jesus walking among the crowds, so pressed upon that he literally feels power going out of him when the sick touch him and receive healing. One priest described accepted practices in the seminary where as a faculty member he lived with the students and could play basketball with them a few hours after hearing their confessions. If as mental health professionals we force our guidelines onto persons in ministry, at worse we will confuse them and at best they will judge our comments as irrelevant.

To understand better the personal and ethical dilemmas that the clergy culture generates for ministers, the experience of the American Psychological Association in creating its most recent ethical guidelines is instructive. After carefully drafting strong and clear ethical statements about psychologists not engaging in dual relationships, the committee was bombarded by objections from psychologists in rural areas. How, they asked, are we to maintain boundaries when we have to treat the daughter of the only lawyer or gynecologist in town? What are we supposed to do when we need their services in return? Are we supposed to violate the principle of not abandoning our clients? How, further, are we to observe the ethical principle of not bartering for our services in a farm economy during drought or crop failure? The Psychological Association had to adapt its guidelines to allow psychologists to use judgment in such circumstances.

What is the exception in mental health is the norm for many religious professionals. How then should therapists help their clients reflect on these issues? First, client and therapist need to collaborate on a boundary assessment. In the chapters on stress and anxiety we have repeatedly discussed the importance of life-style balance. Boundary issues will make the most sense when discussed in light of this broad needs assessment. In this way the discussion revolves around the best way to be helpful to ministers rather than describing rules they may have violated. Ask clients how they have come to feel weary, set upon, in need of refuge. From this discussion the discerning clinician will spot boundaries gone awry.

A comprehensive needs assessment allows the clinician to inquire exactly how the minister is attending to emotional needs. Experience with the whole range of impaired professionals from therapists to attorneys to clergy suggests that the highest risk to public endangerment is when ordinary needs go unmet in the helper. Medical researchers, to insure that they are conducting themselves in an ethical manner, ask a simple question to determine if a procedure is experimental or clinical. Imagine that the patient asks the following question: "Doctor, is what you are doing for me or for you?" There is no getting around the meaning of the procedure when framed in this manner. If ministers could imagine the same question asked by their members, they would gain insight into which part of their work is for themselves and which part for others.

Our experience with boundary violations across professional groups highlights a single observation: *the average boundary violation seldom occurs because the helper intended the outcome;* rather, most result from *the initial, unwise decision to form the particular relationship.* Time after time we see the final quandary as the result of an inevitable unfolding instead of malice. Helping clients become aware of the meaning of these initial decisions to enter a particular relationship will help them prevent many awkward, if not tragic outcomes. What does it mean if I decide to become emotionally involved with this family? Confide in this person? Go on vacation with this couple? Loan, borrow, or accept money? Although sexual boundary violations garnish the biggest headlines, the overwhelming number of violations are small and painful. Unwise initial decisions, then, give way to another ethical principle, that of the slippery slope.

Deacon Sam is an eager, energetic man in his late thirties, flush with his first assignment to a parish. Pastor Phil has asked Sam to focus on the needs of the elderly in the parish. Sam begins by taking a survey at the parish recreation center for the elderly and tabulates the results. He discovers that many are concerned about financial issues in retirement. Sam, an accountant in his full-time work, sets up a seminar on finances for retirement and brings in a financial analyst from Sam's own firm who specializes in this field. The three meetings are well attended and over the course of the meetings Sam discovers that many of the parish elderly are not well-served by their brokers. They are paying far too much in commissions and have overinvested in products that benefit the financial institutions much more than the client. The parishioners come to understand this and many ask him and his firm to help manage their funds. At first, he refuses, but they insist saying that, as a deacon, they know they can trust him. Sam agrees and everyone is happy when rates of return increase dramatically.

If this turns out disastrously, it will not be due to anyone's bad intent. Disaster will strike from some unforeseen circumstance: the bond market collapses, another member of the firm embezzles funds, an irate relative who has power of attorney is excluded. Then everyone will analyze the situation as an unprincipled one based on a violation of dual relationships. Our point here is simply that *they rarely start out looking that way.* Vigilance in the form of the capacity to conduct ongoing boundary assessment is required. Therapists can truly provide a life-giving service to ministers by enabling them to reflect on the difficult dilemmas pastoral life throws their way. Boundary assessment, then, becomes a natural process of self-care instead of another ethical demand.

The following are suggested as guidelines for enhancing boundary sensitivity for clergy and religious.

Minimize the Effect of Dual Relationships Where Possible

Do not use persons in the congregation to serve personal needs. The economic incentive to use congregation members for services ranging from haircuts to investment advice is attractive for ministers already on tight budgets. After all, doesn't the Gospel say, "The laborer is worthy of his hire"? Acknowledging that this requires common sense, particularly in rural areas, the minister should minimize excessive entanglements of a financial or personal nature. Soul-sharing is most free when the confidant is not involved occupationally with the minister, and he or she has no vested interest in the outcome. In the case of granting work projects or services to congregational members, ministers should arrange for an independent board or committee to have authority. Sound fiscal policy may require giving a bid or contract to members of the congregation, but ministers should insulate themselves from the ultimate decision. If the work is unsatisfactory or conflicts arise, resolution falls to a body outside of direct pastoral care.

Subtle conflicts arise over smaller favors: seats on the 50-yard line for the sold-out football game; use of a vacation cabin; discount theater tickets, etc. Balancing social civility against a pattern of clerical entitlement requires periodic assessment. Even offering to pay for perks is not sufficient since many benefactors enjoy providing the gifts.

Develop a Consultation–Liaison Relationship with a Mental Health Consultant

Religious professionals who have major authority roles in their congregations or communities, who oversee large staffs or significant budgets, or who have large counseling loads, will benefit from an ongoing consultation relationship with a mental health professional. We are not suggesting therapy for each person in this category. However, periodic but regular contacts with a knowledgeable clinician can prove invaluable. The following represent typical agenda items a monthly meeting might explore: thorny personnel issues, time management skill development, monitoring self-care programs such as exercise or recreation, attending to workaholic concerns, open discussion of boundary issues, policy development, and preparing for new roles or new ministries.

Those going into new ministry situations should negotiate with the community for payment of such services. Mental health consultation can go a long way to prevent burnout. In addition it lessens the need for legal consultation by enhancing a balanced life-style that minimizes boundary violations, intentional or otherwise.

In our experience this consultation work is among the most gratifying services we provide. Results are almost immediate in terms of clarifying options for the client and preventing mistakes. Clients appreciate the practical nature of the consultation and even leaders who are not psychologically minded benefit. Therapists, of course, need to define with the client the nature of the relationship. A therapeutic relationship oriented toward uncovering and growth may shift into one of professional consultation. This shift, however, requires processing with the client to maintain informed consent.

Also, therapists need to consider the consultation modality that the client requests. For example, a pastor might ask the mental health consultant to attend a parish staff meeting as facilitator. A previous therapeutic relationship between the consultant and the pastor creates a dual relationship for the therapist, which may impede the ability to facilitate the meeting. The consultant does not want to fall into the trap of becoming a negative role model and violate boundaries the consultation relationship was meant to support.

Aggressively Monitor Dependency Needs

Clinical experience and research, as reviewed in the previous chapter, indicate that ministers are most at risk as a result of their own unmet dependency needs. Therapy needs to function as a training ground for ongoing assessment, monitoring, and resolution of unmet needs for personal friendship or other attachments. The therapist can provide no greater service than by assisting clients in preserving integrity and self-care. Developing intimacy and healthy attachments is the major buffer against depression and loneliness, and by extension, the best predictor of maintaining healthy limits within ministry. Intimacy needs are not eliminated, moreover, simply because a minister is married. Indeed, a bad marriage will heighten this need, inasmuch as rates of depression in distressed marriages run about 50% (Beach, Sandeen, & O'Leary, 1990). We discuss strategies for accomplishing this task in several places, particularly chapters 1, 2, 4, and 8.

Develop Effective Supervisor Relationships

Unfortunately supervision in ministry is often a paper exercise, a line drawn on an organizational chart to fulfill an abstract principle. In reality many new in ministry have meager supervision, if any at all. The model used in most ministry situations is the same as that facetiously ascribed to medical training: "See one, do one, teach one." Several barriers exist to effective supervision. First, many institutions do not value the supervisory process. The nominal supervisor is the already overworked leader who is swamped with major pastoral or administrative responsibilities. In this setup supervision is an afterthought. Here the organizational structure does not permit either supervisor or supervisee with the requisite time.

Second, most ministry leaders themselves are unskilled in the art of supervision. Trained as they were in the learn-by-doing model, they do not typically reflect on the process of transmitting skills, an essential ingredient in effective supervision. Some leaders are naturally gifted supervisors, but in these instances, again, the system does not support their gifts with the necessary resources. Historically, mental health training is equally deficient regarding formal course work in supervision. Despite attaining doctoral clinical degrees in psychology, for example, neither author's program offered courses in how to supervise. Psychology, of course, is quite supervision intensive in fieldwork, practicums, and internships; but interestingly, it is expected that this skill will develop by osmosis. Ministry training has a double whammy, having no training in how to supervise, and additionally providing little supervision to fledgling religious professionals. Almost all helping professionals require a minimum of 2 years intense supervision *post-degree* before they get their credentials. Ongoing training in ministry is rare, except for those who enter specialized ministries. Most religious institutions require no continuing education for generalists. As one religious leader was fond of saying, "The average parish priest obtains his ongoing theology training from the religion section of *Time* magazine." For many ministers both practical and theoretical training ends upon their first assignment. Only those in professions that require independent credentials have built-in growth programs.

A therapist needs to identify when supervision might enhance the client's effectiveness and recommend obtaining it. Here, too, therapists should encourage clients to seek remuneration for such assistance from the community ministered to as one of the costs for effective pastoral care. Faith communities need to factor in as essential support the costs of supervision and mental health consultation-liaison as an important prophylactic against burnout and boundary violations. Or, in the words of a parish team member, parishes require more intentionality in the care and feeding of their ministers.

Pastoral Counseling Should Be Short Term

For ministers without formal counseling credentials, counseling within the faith community needs to adhere to structured time limits. Routine pastoral care should encompass no more than a few sessions for assessment, a few sessions for intervention, then referral for work on long-term issues. Agreed-upon time-limits minimize the transference–countertransference issues that trigger boundary violations in the unwary or unskilled. Trained pastoral counselors also want to avoid long-term counseling with members of their own faith communities. This reduces awkwardness that may result from future dual relationships, e.g., when the counselor must function in a different role such as parish administrator or school board member.

TRANSITIONS

Overview

In his high school graduation address the local school superintendent told the graduates they would likely change careers, not just jobs, eight times before retirement. Adults in the audience reacted visibly to this statement with many silently counting on their fingers their own career changes. A woman, who was only in her fifties, looked amazed and held up five fingers to her partner verifying the speaker's statement.

Career change is an equal fact of life in ministry as in all walks of modern life. In the late 1960s and entire 1970s an enormous change took place in the Roman Catholic priesthood when thousands left to pursue a secular life. Around this same era Catholic sisters and brothers also left their religious communities in great numbers. Protestant ministry had always been fluid with regard to transition with its social structure of churches calling its ministers (i.e., a public announcement of a church's need for a pastor). In this system a call is not guaranteed nor is it a lifetime condition. Ministers often move freely back and forth between religious and secular occupations.

Transfers, moreover, are a way of life in ministry much as they are in military service. Individuals and families are accustomed to moving every few years. Most are adept at coping with these changes. The grown daughter of a Baptist minister brags that she and her mother could pack an entire household on 36-hours notice. Some of the stresses discussed below also apply to *transfer,* but transfer does not usually provoke the same degree of emotional stress as full transition. Formal and informal welcoming systems operate in ministry groups to cushion the change and help the new person and his or her family adapt.

In this section we explore the psychological issues involved in transitions according to type. We discuss (1) permanent transition from ministry to lay life; (2) leave of absence transitions; (3) role transition within ministry; and (4) retirement. Before discussing the particulars of each transition we need to discuss the general topic of discernment.

Discernment

In this setting discernment refers to the decision process in transition. Psychotherapy will often provide an important ingredient in discernment so the forces prevailing upon the individual client are worth examining.

The first consideration is to assess the driving force behind discernment. How is the question of transition arising? What drives it? Broadly speaking, although the categories can intermingle, transition involves predominantly a *leaving for* or a *leaving from.* In the first instance the person identifies something or someone that is positive and presumably will fill up one's life. In the discernment process of leaving-for, attitudes toward the institution will vary. Some will be indifferent, some will retain an attachment, and others will experience rejection if they cannot remain in good standing with their institution. In these instances the stresses are related to coping with adaptive changes to one's environment rather than binding up one's emotional wounds.

Leaving-from represents a different reality. This occurs in the context of burnout, depression, discouragement or even failure. One gets out for the sake of sheer survival. Emotional sequelae here relate to self-esteem issues. In no particular order the likely feelings are poor self-esteem, reduced self-efficacy, depression, future-directed anxiety, and rage or bitterness toward one's former way of life. Leaving-from represents greater emotional distress than leaving-for. A sense of incompleteness or futility about wasted years may haunt the client. Religious professionals in the leaving-for category often view their ministry as a genuine call from God, one that prepared them for their next stage in life's journey. The process of psychotherapy may help religious develop alternative perspectives, and help those in the leaving-from category view their ministry and themselves in a less negative light. When so many Catholic clergy and religious left in the 1960s, some spiritual writers coined the term *temporary vocation* to change the negative views of these persons as "Judas," "apostates," or persons who "couldn't keep their vows." What social reality did for theological understanding, psychotherapy can accomplish for personal understanding. Transition in ministry is so common today that the former extremes of social opprobrium are rare. One of us recalls a sermon 25 years ago on Holy Thursday, the feast of the Eucharist, and for many Christians the establishment of priesthood. The priest asked the people to reflect on and appreciate the fidelity of their priests, "Unlike all those priests who have left and cannot honor their commitments to God." Even though society may not denigrate clergy and religious in transition, the individual may play that role himself or herself. This is more likely when no vision beyond ministry but only the pain *of* ministry motivates the departure.

Clinicians need to attend to depression masking itself as a career crisis. Although depression may be an important signal to reevaluate suitability for ministry, aggressive treatment of depression is essential prior to any permanent decision. The natural symptoms of depression, self-denigration, pessimism about the future, disbelief in one's personal abilities, etc., all may disguise themselves as reasons for leaving ministry.

Leaving Ministry

In discernment about leaving ministry the client naturally weighs the pros and cons. Therapy assists that process with the advantage of having a neutral advocate in the therapist. One issue so permeates transition for Roman Catholic clergy, brothers and sisters, that it requires separate discussion: leaving ministry over the issue of required celibacy. Some men and women who initially accept celibacy as part of their religious ministry eventually view it as burdensome. For these individuals psychotherapy is a reflective process to help them discern their eventual career choice. Many will have already reflected on this with mentors or spiritual directors. At least two situations are common during this process and each represents a different therapeutic challenge.

Intimacy Involvement

The first occurs when the client has fallen in love and is in a reciprocal intimate relationship, whether or not they have initiated sexual activity. We are assuming here that the partner is not a counselee or from a pastoral helping relationship that involves a boundary violation. Under the circumstances of reciprocal love the client must reflect on two separate issues: (1) Do I want to make a commitment to this person; and (2) even if I do not, what is the meaning of my experience ultimately in terms of my vow of celibacy? We have addressed many of the questions surrounding celibate commitment in chapter 8 and will not repeat them. Here we want to reflect on the psychological issues should the client decide to leave ministry as a result of pursuing a romantic relationship that precludes remaining in ministry. Although this issue may seem to refer only to Roman Catholic clergy and vowed religious, the situation may relate to other groups as well. For example, in some denominations a homosexual minister who chooses to live publicly in a committed sexual relationship cannot remain in active ministry.

The major problem for discernment under these circumstances is the restrictions placed on the relationships due to the minister's public life. Think of the phases in an average courtship. Most people never attend to the critical importance of openness and the freedom to move about in public. Imagine trying to get to know a person, but you can only observe that person's behavior in a narrowly confined space, e.g., a cottage on a lake or in their apartment. Although this confinement may lead to your acquiring many details through conversation, you may not learn what this person is like in other important social environments: with other couples, at a party, in the presence of romantic rivals, around children, or significant family members. Most of all you do not get the opportunity to see or test out how it feels to be in a relationship in these different circumstances. Furthermore, the initial stage of intense romantic attachment amplifies the partner's idealistic qualities preventing the normal introduction of reality that comes from exposure to multiple social settings.

Religious professionals in love fail to appreciate the artificiality surrounding these developing relationships or to take into account how much interpersonal behavior gets lost as a result. Decisions based on so few observations of a partner's behavior are as open to error for the same reason as statistical studies with small samples. A homosexual relationship heightens further this artificiality resulting from the need for secrecy.

The only antidote for this situation is time. To minimize making a poor judgment the client should give more time than seems reasonable to establishing the strength of the relationship. Many pressures conspire against this: the intensity of the attraction, the partner demanding a decision, a pending transfer, and even fear of discovery. When the relationship suffers from secrecy yet a decision to leave ensues, the therapist needs to point out the importance of moving into a new phase of discovery. The single worse mistake such couples make is to commit immediately to the relationship upon leaving ministry. The wisest, if seldom adhered to, advice is to play the field, get to know the person more casually, see other people. Religious professionals usually have the greater conflict and are less likely to know their minds than their partners. This sets up a tension in the relationship because they require time to shake the artificial dating environment in ministry. Their partners, on the other hand, have tested the waters for some time. When they hear from the minister, "We need to go slow," or "I need more time," experience tells them these are code words for commitment phobia. Naturally they would press for stronger reassurance. Ministers with strong dependency needs cannot easily negotiate the importance of taking time with its risk of disappointing their partners. Yet nothing is more crucial.

Loss Issues

Independent from or concomitant with intimacy factors in transition are myriad losses. Preparing the client for these losses can minimize their impact and provide a signal mechanism to activate prearranged coping strategies. Perhaps the saddest loss surrounds friendship. Despite protestations on all sides, leaving the total environment of a religious community forever affects the majority of friendships. This does not mean that a few cherished friendships will not endure or that some cannot reconstitute themselves, but many warm relationships pass forever. This falling away rarely results from bad intentions or indifference. Rather, it results from leaving a single-focus environment shared by committed people. That environment determines people's interests, goals, and motivation. Similar friendship fading occurs following college graduation, leaving the military, or the end of an intensive training experience.

Former religious professionals are often not in tune with transference phenomena. As a therapist you are totally familiar with the projections clients place on you. Ministers can fail to appreciate how much interpersonal dynamics result from projections toward them. Their high social status, the intense, durable, and frequent expressions of warmth extended them, all derive as much from their role as their personality. When the role goes, so do the projections.

Closely related to friendship loss is loss of social status. More than one ex-minister has noted how no one ever calls them to come to the head of the line when purchasing tickets to an event or waiting in a restaurant. Being "one of the troops" means missing out on various perks that buffered financial deprivations associated with ministerial work.

During transition many will not move into a satisfying occupation immediately. Most will be underemployed in positions considerably below their educational qualifications. Keeping this status in perspective requires considerable emotional balance.

Jerry, a 28-year-old Methodist minister, recently left his associate pastor position to pursue a relationship with a man he was in love with. A recession in the economy meant that he was grateful to have a part-time job in a large chain grocery store which, because of union benefits, meant he could at least eat and pay rent while pursuing full-time job leads. He had a number of encounters that always left him feeling sad for the loss of personal and professional recognition that he had enjoyed as a young, popular minister in his church. When customer flow was down the assistant store managers would ask him to mop up breakages in the food aisles or other tasks instead of his main job checking-out groceries. He did not think mopping floors was beneath his dignity, but the contrast in job satisfaction between handling broken baby food jars and having worshippers praise his sermon was demoralizing. On a bitterly cold Christmas eve he was asked to work pick-up outside, placing grocery bags in customer cars. A late model Cadillac pulled up driven by a woman who did not need to get out of the car because she could control the trunk with an automatic button inside. As Jerry placed the many bags into her trunk he couldn't help but notice that the trunk carpet was a finer grade and quality than he could afford in his apartment. When he finished the woman beckoned to him through the back windshield. As he approached she rolled down the power window and gave him a nickel, saying, "Have a merry Christmas, Sonny." With the sleet falling heavily he suppressed an intense urge to wave his arm in righteous protest screaming, "You bastard, don't you know I have a master's degree?"

Others in transition will encounter practical life issues from which religious life or training may have shielded them. When she opened her first checking account at age 35, a former nun needed to have a very young bank clerk show her how to write a check. Some may never have lived alone, rented an apartment, developed a budget, bought a car, or ordered telephone service. Whatever their chronological age it is useful to think of this phase as developmentally similar to that of a young adult leaving home for the first time. Mentors in the form of family and friends can play a similar role for the minister in transition.

Vocational Transition

The job search is usually the immediate pressing problem. If at all possible, follow the adage that the best time to look for a job is when you already have one. Suggest to clients that they not leave ministry completely until they have lined up a replacement. Clinical consultation can facilitate this process. First, a resumé must be constructed. Even ministers who have worked in their field for decades may not have any resumé. Putting the resumé together is therapeutic because it forces clients to translate their job skills for the secular workplace. Ministers are often unaware that many pastoral tasks translate into Department of Labor classification titles. Being pastor of a church translates into many administrative headings from budget development, personnel selection, staff training, purchasing, record keeping, and even school administration. Human services are the most directly translated especially those involving counseling, group dynamics, conflict resolution, and the like.

Clinicians may want to refer clients in transition to a specialized career counseling center. Vocational and psychological assessment may suggest occupations that clients would otherwise ignore. Some regions even have career guidance programs that specialize in ministry transition. A comprehensive assessment would include interview, resumé writing, skill training, vocational testing, and personality testing. If the client has specialized interests aptitude tests are also available.

With or without formal assessment, therapists can focus clients on the usual practices in career development. In addition to resumé writing, clients need to put together their list of contacts for interviewing. Clergy and religious often have a large available pool of contacts. In our experience most are willing to help. Again, an adage from career guidance is useful here: never meet with anyone without getting from that person the names of at least three other people to contact. Most effective in reducing the natural anxiety around the job search is making clients go on abundant interviews, even those they are not interested in or for which they have no qualifications. Interviews and role-playing will train them to perfect their pitch and deal with their perceived embarrassment should interviewers raise the issue of their previous career. Standard role-playing can help by asking clients the questions they most fear. Fantasies of rejection or ridicule quickly dissipate for one of two reasons. Most Americans are churchgoers and harbor little animosity toward clergy. Second, many job interviewers have met former ministers and know they are good workers. One applicant discovered that an entire office of a federal regulatory agency consisted of former clergy, nuns, and monks.

RETIREMENT

Generalizations about retirement are impossible when one considers the immense differences between and within religious cultures. On the issue of financial resources alone a few examples should suffice. Members of mainstream Protestant congregations may have retirement funds invested by the central administration that rival those in business. Assuming eligibility for Social Security and federal health insurance programs, these combined financial programs should at least prevent poverty in old age. Members of small congregations will have fewer resources and will need to have self-insured programs, either from outside work sources or private savings.

In Catholicism the situation is quite different. For priests who are members of regional groups (dioceses), retirement support will come from priests' retirement funds based on meager base salaries. Room and board in retirement is usually guaranteed, either through residence in a parish rectory or in a sponsored nursing home. Priests who have independent financial resources from private earnings or family inheritance may choose to live independently or with family and friends. For male members of religious communities, retirement may mean living in a special retirement residence or some living arrangement approved by the superior. Again, room and board are usually provided. Women religious operate under considerable financial handicaps. For generations sisters operated the Catholic school system for which they received salaries well below half of their equally educated lay peers. Observing the vow of poverty meant that individual sisters received a small monthly personal allowance with the remainder going to the community's governing budget to support training, health care, administrative costs, missionary, and uncompensated charitable work. As a result they were not legally permitted to make personal contributions into the government's Social Security retirement system. When the law changed to allow individual members to participate, many communities did not have the huge lump sums required to qualify their members for retroactive eligibility. This requires many communities, whose majority membership is elderly, to depend on outside support to fund retirement.

As a result the situation of elderly religious women, and some men, has reached crisis proportions. With reduced admissions into religious life, the average age of communities in some cases reaches above 60 years old. With minimal or no Social Security benefits, fewer members of salaried age, and skyrocketing health care costs, the ability of communities to be self-sustaining has plummeted. Many are selling off assets simply to meet basic costs. At the same time, some women religious have developed model retirement programs to meet psychological needs. Most sisters in retirement communities receive ample human contact and live as independently as health permits.

Except for the seriously ill and the very old, retirement is an abstraction with members feeling pressured to stay in the work force as long as possible. In the United States the priest shortage has created a similar situation. Some dioceses refuse to accept any healthy priest's retirement before age 75.

These issues for Catholic clergy, then, mean therapists will have to assess the restrictions placed on their elderly clients. Sometimes the therapeutic task will be coping with *not* retiring, a task that is countercultural to our society. Feature stories of the very old working are a commonplace for sisters and brothers. While their ability to work is commendable, the issue for therapy is whether or not the choice is voluntary.

Gerontology specialists with clergy and religious say the word *retirement* has a pejorative meaning with this population. Maryknoll priest and gerontologist Ed Killacky (personal communication) relates this to the tradition of personal self-denial. When self-denial, rather than self-esteem, drives one's life, retirement presents special hazards. Self-esteem for many religious professionals revolves totally around one's ministry so that self-worth is something that gets bootstrapped. A self-denial mode means that the person submerges the natural ego enhancement that emerges from a job well done. When the minister can no longer fulfill that job, self-esteem plummets. This link between self-esteem and occupation is one that occurs in the secular world as well, particularly with men. Retirement for religious amplifies this link since many will have no families left for emotional support.

Adjustment to retirement communities creates another strain since many will have never lived in a community before. Communities of nuns and brothers frequently have central retirement facilities which the member may view as "being put on a shelf." In reality they are vibrant and active places in comparison to some geriatric programs in the secular world.

Many groups have come to value psychotherapy for the elderly. Therapists who work with religious professionals should expect to see more referrals from this age group. A developmental model suggests that unresolved psychopathology may rear up during this stage. Prejudices may become more entrenched, entitlement may flourish, civility become nonexistent. Integrating the person's spiritual coping resources at this point is a major path for growth. Can the person rescue hope from despair during this phase? Or, can the person at least learn how to accept hope *in* the despair? The elderly religious are usually open to this self-discovery process when they sense acceptance of spirituality in their listeners. Therapists can invite the client to reexamine spiritual traditions long held but perhaps never applied.

In some instances the elderly remain imprisoned in their own anxiety. As therapists we may fail to see that the elderly person's failure to change occurs because we neglect to encourage the possibilities for growth even with advanced age. In the following example a superior gently encourages a frightened retiree to free himself from chains that had long suppressed his self-expression.

> Father Bill was the General Superior of a large Catholic religious order. He lived in the order's *motherhouse,* which served both as headquarters and a residence for retirees. Bill enjoyed visiting with the elderly in their rooms, and particularly enjoyed hearing their firsthand accounts of the early history of the community settling in the United States from the old country. One day, when visiting Brother Dan, an 89-year-old retired teacher, Tom spied a dusty violin case high up on some shelves in the monk's chambers. Dan admitted he once played well enough to belong to a community concert quartet. When Bill invited Dan to play for him, Dan whispered that he could not. Over 50 years ago a previous superior angrily told Dan he had to stop playing because the noise bothered the other monks. Further, he was told, it was unseemly for a monk to exhibit pleasure in such "worldly" entertainment. Father Bill reminded Dan that Bill was now the superior and insisted that Dan entertain him with his violin. Thereafter the two passed many an afternoon together listening to Mozart.

The summing up that takes place during this life phase requires integrating what they have accomplished in life with the perspective of who they are in relationship to their God. Therapists of any religious or spiritual view will be rewarded for accompanying the religious minister on this most important journey.

References and Suggested Readings

Ainsworth, M. D. S., & Bowlby, J. (1990). An ethological approach to personality development. *American Psychologist, 46,* 333–341.

American Psychiatric Association (1994). *Diagnostic and statistical manual of mental disorders* (4th ed.). Washington, DC: American Psychiatric Press.

Augsburger, D. (1979). *Anger and assertiveness in pastoral care.* Philadelphia: Fortress.

Barlow, D. H. (1988). *Anxiety and its disorders: The nature and treatment of anxiety and panic.* New York: Guilford.

Baumeister, R. F., Heatherton, T. F., & Tice, D. M. (1994). *Losing control: How and why people fail at self-regulation.* New York: Academic Press.

Beach, S. R. H., Sandeen, E. E., & O'Leary, K. D. (1990). *Depression in marriage: A model for etiology and treatment.* New York: Guilford.

Beck, A. T., Freeman, A., & Associates (1990). *Cognitive therapy of personality disorders.* New York: Guilford.

Beck, A. T., Rush, J. Shaw, B., & Emery, G. (1979). *Cognitive therapy of depression.* New York: Guilford.

Bergin, A. E. (1991). Values and religious issues in psychotherapy and mental health. *American Psychologist, 46,* 394–403.

Berry, J. (1992). *Lead us not into temptation: Catholic priests and the sexual abuse of children.* New York: Doubleday.

Blatt, S. J. (1995). The destructiveness of perfectionism: Implications for the treatment of depression. *American Psychologist, 50,* 1003–1020.

Bowlby, J. (1988). *A secure base: Parent–child attachment and healthy human development.* New York: Basic Books.

Bunyan, J. (1988). *Grace abounding: To the chief of sinners.* Westfield, NJ: Christian Library. (Original work published 1666.)

Burns, D. D. (1989). *The feeling good handbook: Using the new mood therapy in everyday life.* New York: William Morrow.

Burwicki, R. (1981). *Anger: Defusing the bomb.* Wheaton, IL: Tyndale.

Carnes, P. (1991). *Don't call it love: Recovery from sexual addiction.* New York: Bantam.

Cheston, S. (1994). *As you and the abused person journey together.* New York: Paulist Press.

Choca, J. P., Shanley, L. A., & Van Denburg, E. (1992). *Interpretative guide to the Millon Clinical Multiaxial Inventory.* Washington, DC: American Psychological Association.

Ciarrocchi, J. W. (1987). Severity of impairment in dually addicted gamblers. *Journal of Gambling Behavior, 3,* 16–26.

Ciarrocchi, J. W. (1991). Counseling the recovering alcoholic. In B. Estadt, J. Compton, & M. Blanchette (Eds.), *Pastoral counseling* (2nd ed., pp. 243–259). New York: Prentice-Hall.

Ciarrocchi, J. W. (1992). Pathological gambling and pastoral counseling. In R. J. Wicks, R. D. Parsons, & D. E. Capps (Eds.), *Clinical handbook of pastoral counseling* (Vol. 2; pp. 593–620). New York: Paulist Press.

Ciarrocchi, J. W. (1995a). *The doubting disease: Help for scrupulosity and religious compulsions.* New York: Paulist Press.

Ciarrocchi, J. W. (1995b). *Why are you worrying?* New York: Paulist Press.

Ciarrocchi, J. W. (1998). Religion, scrupulosity, and obsessive-compulsive disorder. In M. A. Jenike, L. Baer, & W. E. Minichiello (Eds.), *Obsessive–compulsive disorders: Practical management* (3rd ed., pp. 555–569). St. Louis: Mosby.

Ciarrocchi, J. W., & Hohmann, A. (1989). The family environment of married male pathological gamblers, alcoholics, and dually addicted gamblers. *Journal of Gambling Behavior, 5,* 283–291.

Ciarrocchi, J. W., & Reinert, D. (1993). Family environment and length of recovery for married members of Gamblers Anonymous. *Journal of Gambling Studies, 9,* 341–352.

Costa, P. T., Jr., & McCrae, R. R. (1992). *Revised NEO Personality Inventory: Professional manual.* Odessa, FL: Psychological Assessment Resources.

Craske, M. G., Barlow, D. H., & O'Leary, T. (1992). *Mastery of your anxiety and worry.* Albany, NY: Graywind.

Crosby, M. (1996). *Celibacy: Means of control or mandate of the heart?* Notre Dame, IN: Ave Maria.

Custer, R., & Milt, H. (1985). *When luck runs out: Help for compulsive gamblers and their families.* New York: Facts on File.

Davison, G. C. (1976). Homosexuality: The ethical challenge. *Journal of Consulting and Clinical Psychology, 44,* 157–162.

Ellis, A. (1983). *The case against religion.* New York: The Institute for Rational-Emotive Therapy.

Ellis, A., & Harper, R. (1975). *A new guide to rational living.* North Hollywood, CA: Wilshire Books.

Flaherty, S. (1992). *Woman, why do you weep? Spirituality for adult survivors of sexual abuse.* New York: Paulist Press.

Fox, M. (1972). *On becoming a musical mystical bear.* New York: Paulist Press.

Goergen, D. (1979). *The sexual celibate.* New York: Image.

Gonsiorek, J. C. (Ed.). (1995). *Breach of trust: Sexual exploitation by health care professionals and clergy.* Thousand Oaks, CA: Sage.

Greenberg, D. (1984). Are religious compulsions religious or compulsive? *American Journal of Psychotherapy, 38,* 524–532.

Hammett, R., & Sofield, L. (1981). *Inside the Christian community.* New York: LeJacq.

Hayes, S. C. (1994). Content, context, and the types of psychological acceptance. In S. C. Hayes, N. S. Jacobson, V. M. Follette, & M. J. Dougher (Eds.), *Acceptance and change: Content and context in psychotherapy.* Reno, NV: Context Press.

Hoge, D. (1996). Religion in America. In E. P. Shafranske (Ed.), *Religion and the clinical practice of psychology* (pp. 21–42). Washington, DC: American Psychological Association.

Johnson, V. (1980). *I'll quit tomorrow* (Rev. ed.). New York: Harper & Row.

Kabat-Zinn, J. (1990). *Full catastrophe living: Using the wisdom of your body and mind to face stress, pain, and illness.* New York: Delta Press.

Kaufmann, W. (1973). *Without guilt and justice: From decidophobia to autonomy.* New York: Peter H. Wyden.

Klerman, G. L., Weissman, M. M., Rounsaville, B. J., & Chevron, E. S. (1984). *Interpersonal psychotherapy of depression.* New York: Basic Books.

Lakein, A. (1973). *How to get control of your time and your life.* New York: New American Library.

Langer, E. J. (1989). *Mindfulness.* Reading, MA: Addison-Wesley.

Linehan, M. (1993). *Skills training manual for treating borderline personality disorder.* New York: Guilford.

LoPiccolo, J. (1994). Acceptance and broad spectrum treatment of paraphilias. In S. C. Hayes, N. S. Jacobson, V. M. Follette, & M. J. Dougher (Eds.), *Acceptance and change: Content and context in psychotherapy* (pp. 149–170). Reno, NV: Context Press.

Mahoney, D. (1991). *Touching the face of God: Intimacy and celibacy in priestly life.* Boca Raton, FL: Jeremiah Press.

Marlatt, G. A. (1994). Addiction and acceptance. In S. C. Hayes, N. S. Jacobson, V. M. Follette, & M. Dougher (Eds.), *Acceptance and change: Content and context in psychotherapy* (pp. 175–197). Reno, NV: Context Press.

Masters, W. H., & Johnson, V. E. (1970). *Human sexual inadequacy.* Boston: Little, Brown.

Meichenbaum, D., & Cameron, R. (1983). Stress inoculation training: Toward a general paradigm for training coping skills. In D. Meichenbaum & M. E. Jaremko (Eds.), *Stress reduction and prevention* (pp. 115–154). New York: Plenum.

Mickey, P., & Gamble, G. (1978). *Pastoral assertiveness: A new model for pastoral care.* Nashville, TN: Abingdon.

Miller, W. R., & Rollnick, S. (Eds.). (1991). *Motivational interviewing: Preparing people to change addictive behavior.* New York: Guilford.

Millon, T. (1983). *Millon Clinical Multiaxial Inventory manual* (3rd ed.). Minneapolis, MN: National Computer Systems.

Murphy, S. (1992). *A delicate dance.* New York: Crossroad.

The New American Bible (1988). (Rev. ed.). Mission Hills, CA: Benzinger.

Nugent, C. D., Gill, J. P., & Plaut, S. M. (Eds.). (1996). *Sexual exploitation: Strategies for prevention and intervention. Report of the Maryland Task Force to Study Heath Professional–Client Sexual Exploitation.* Baltimore: Maryland Department of Health & Mental Hygiene.

Parsons, R., & Wicks, R. (Eds.). (1983). *Passive-aggressiveness: Theory and practice.* New York: Brunner/Mazel.

Pearlman, L. A., & MacIan, P. S. (1995). Vicarious traumatization: An empirical study of the effects of trauma work on trauma therapists. *Professional Psychology: Research and Practice, 26,* 558–565.

Perls, F. S., Hefferline, R. F., & Goodman, P. (1951). *Gestalt therapy.* New York: Julian Press.

Piedmont, R. L. (1998). *The revised NEO-Personality Inventory: Clinical and research applications.* New York: Plenum.

Project Match Research Group (1997). Matching alcoholism treatments to client heterogeneity: Project MATCH posttreatment drinking outcomes. *Journal of Studies on Alcohol, 58,* 7–29.

Propst, L. T., Ostrom, R., Watkins, P., Dean, T., & Masburn, D. (1992). Comparative efficacy of religious and non-religious cognitive-behavioral therapy for the treatment of clinical depression in religious individuals. *Journal of Consulting and Clinical Psychology, 60,* 94–103.

Rodgerson, T. (1994). *Spirituality, stress and you.* New York: Paulist Press.

Rutter, P. (1989). *Sex in the forbidden zone.* New York: Fawcett Crest.

Schoener, G. (1995). Assessment of professionals who have engaged in boundary violations. *Psychiatric Annals, 2,* 95–99.

Sipe, A. W. R. (1990). *A secret world: Sexuality and the search for celibacy.* New York: Brunner/Mazel.

Steketee, G., Quay, S., & White, K. (1991). Religion and guilt in OCD patients. *Journal of Anxiety Disorders, 5,* 359–367.

Steketee, G., & White, K. (1990). *When once is not enough: Help for obsessive compulsives.* Oakland, CA: New Harbinger.

Sullivan, H. S. (1953). *The interpersonal theory of psychiatry.* New York: Norton.

Taylor, G. (1996). *An empirical comparison of intermittent and compulsive sexually exploitative clergy.* Unpublished doctoral dissertation, Loyola College in Maryland.

Thompson, F. (1958). The hound of heaven. In R. Aldington (Ed.), *The Viking book of poetry of the English-speaking world* (Vol. 2). New York: Viking.

Wegner, D. (1989). *White bears and other unwanted thoughts: Suppression, obses-sion, and the psychology of mental control.* New York: Viking.

Wicks, R. (1983). Passive-aggressiveness within the religious setting. In R. Parsons & R. Wicks (Eds.), *Passive-aggressiveness: Theory and practice* (pp. 213–227). New York: Brunner/Mazel.

Wicks, R. (1986). *Availability: The problem and the gift.* New York: Paulist Press.

Wicks, R. (1990). *Self-ministry through self-understanding.* Chicago: Loyola University Press.

Wicks, R. (1991). *Seeking perspective.* New York: Paulist Press.

Wicks, R. (1993). Countertransference and burnout. In R. Wicks, R. Parsons, & D. E. Capps (Eds.), *Clinical handbook of pastoral counseling.* Vol. 1 (Expanded ed., pp. 76–96). New York: Paulist Press.

Wicks, R. (1994). *Touching the holy.* Notre Dame, IN: Ave Maria.

Wicks, R. (1995a). *Seeds of sensitivity.* Notre Dame, IN: Ave Maria.

Wicks, R. (1995b). The stress of spiritual ministry: Practical suggestions on avoiding unnecessary distress. In R. Wicks (Ed.), *Handbook of spiritual-ity for ministers* (pp. 256–258). New York: Paulist Press.

Yalom, I. D. (1995). *The theory and practice of group psychotherapy* (4th ed.). New York: Basic Books.